MOM RULES

Notes on Motherhood, the World's Best Job

Jill Milligan with Michael Milligan

Illustrations by Adam Wallenta

Skyhorse Publishing

Skyhorse Publishing books may be purchased in bulk at special discounts for
sales promotion, corporate gifts, fund-raising, or educational purposes. Special
editions can also be created to specifications. For details, contact the Special Sales
Department, Skyhorse Publishing, 307 West 36th Street, Floor 11, New York, New
York 10018 or info@skyhorsepublishing.com.

www.skyhorsepublishing.com

10 9 8 7 6 5 4 3 2 1

Library of Congress Cataloging-in-Publication Data

Milligan, Jill.
  Mom rules : notes on motherhood, the world's best job / Jill and Michael
Milligan ; illustrations by Adam Wallenta.
     p. cm.
 1. Motherhood. I. Milligan, Michael, 1947- II. Wallenta, Adam. III. Title.
  HQ759.M594 2010
  649'.10852--dc22

                                    2009050524

Print ISBN: 978-1-62873-778-3

Cover design by Danielle Ceccolini

Printed in China

CONTENTS

PREFACE

M*om Rules* is dedicated to the proposition that all men are created equal. And that all women are created way beyond equal, because women are the ones entrusted with the world's most important job: being a mom.

If you think that we're overstating the importance of motherhood, consider that without moms, there'd be no dads. And without dads, who would moms poke fun at? Without moms, there would be no children. And without children, there'd be no messy garages, college tuition, or Pee-Wee Herman.

Mom Rules is based on personal experiences and insight as well as the unique and humorous experiences of scores of moms we talked to in writing this book. Their unique and loose "rules," plus their off-center perspective on the joys of motherhood, are guaranteed to put a smile on your face.

For example, here's a Mom Rule from J. B. Whitney of California: "If you want to expand the variety of foods your kids are willing to eat, send them to someone else's house."

And this rule comes from Carolyn Schmidt of Vermont: "Make your kids take naps for as many years as you can. When they get too old for daily naps, call it 'quiet time.' When they're too old for 'quiet time,' call it 'mom time' and install a lock on your bedroom door."

But we didn't limit our interviews solely to moms, because the title *Mom Rules* has another implication. We also talked to children of all ages and asked them to complete the following sentence: "My mom rules because_____."

Here are a couple of their responses:

"My mom rules because she's kind and unique," said nine-year-old Adrian Enzastiga of Nebraska.

And here's why eight-year-old Morgan McIntyre says she has the best mom in the world: "My mom rules because she can't cook and we get to eat out a lot!"

So, whether you're a woman considering motherhood or an expectant mom, a new mom, a longtime mom, a married mom, a single mom, a step mom, or even an octomom, you'll quickly see that *Mom Rules* offers a loving look at both familiar and unique styles of mothering.

Finally, we believe that *Mom Rules* can be best enjoyed once the kids are asleep, the laundry is done, and your significant other is in front of the big screen, his eyes glued to *Monster Tractor Pull* or something equally challenging. So put your feet up, enjoy a cool glass of your favorite beverage, and it won't be long before you'll see that no matter what Dad may say, the evidence is indisputable: Mom Rules.

ONE

A WORD OF CAUTION

Before we go any further, you should know that there is one disconcerting aspect of motherhood that separates it from every other important profession. This cold, hard fact is not pretty; but, alas, it's true. To become a mom, a woman needs absolutely no qualifications or prior training. Consider . . .

To become a doctor, one needs to not only navigate the physical and intellectual rigors of medical school, but also put in at least two additional years of internships before receiving a license to practice medicine. Likewise, a lawyer must complete law school, and then pass a demanding and highly competitive exam to be admitted to the bar. And an undergraduate degree and at least one year of student teaching is required before one is certified as an educator.

Now consider this . . .

Women take many different roads to motherhood: some of us wait until we meet Mister Perfect; others insist on financial and professional security before even considering having a child. But no matter what our motivation, the sobering truth is that all we *really* need to become a mother is a cheap bottle of wine and someone to whisper, "Of course I love you."

And then, several weeks later, we have to be able to pee on a stick.

Can you imagine the kind of world it would be if other important professions operated under such lax standards? What if the only training required to become a police officer were presenting an oral critique of an episode of *Cops* and passing a blind taste test to identify various types of donuts? And what if, when we were hospitalized, the person providing us with TLC were allowed to become a registered nurse simply because in her high school yearbook she wrote: "I, like, so totally want to help people."

And would anyone ever get on a commercial airliner if "Sully" Sullenberger earned his wings simply because he never gets airsick? Or because he looks really cool in a uniform? Don't think so.

So although motherhood ranks at the top of the importance scale, it seems to be the only critical profession in which no first-hand understanding or experience is necessary—or possible—until after you become a mother. And don't fool yourself into thinking that you gained all the mothering experience you need just because you used to babysit your little brother when you were a teenager. Warning a four-year-old that he better stop his whining while you're on the phone with your boyfriend or you'll use his Lincoln Logs for firewood does not necessarily make you mom-ready.

Of course, there are pre-mom courses that are intended to teach moms-to-be what to expect. Birthing classes can teach you important breathing techniques that will help you during labor and delivery. What birthing classes *cannot* do is guarantee that you'll remember these techniques when the moment arrives and you feel like one elephant is jumping on your uterus while another one is kicking to get out. And though wearing a pregnancy suit can give you a taste of what walking around with a fifty-pound water balloon in your midsection might feel like, try wearing it 24/7, like when you have to get out of a chair. Or use the toilet. Then, add to this the fact that by now, your feet have expanded to the size of Big Foot's, and you're only getting *close* to what it's all about.

So although there is really nothing to accurately prepare you for the act of childbirth, we've developed a few experiments you can try before your baby is born—or even before you choose to become pregnant—to experience what your perfectly calm and tranquil life will be like once a very little version of you begins calling you "Mommy."

The first of these requires that you grab your tape recorder and go to your local kiddie pizza restaurant. If you do not know where one of these is located in your town, simply look for a big neon sign reading PIZZA AND GAMES. If the parking lot is full of pickup trucks and men carrying pool cues, keep going until you find a parking lot crammed with SUVs with child safety seats in back. Go inside and grab a table right in the middle of the action (i.e., somewhere between the video games and the juggling clown). Then take out your tape recorder, set it on the table, and begin recording with the volume all the way up so you can get the full impact of the piercing shrieks of young children. "Mommy, look what I can do!" several bellow. "Mommy, Jimmy made soda come out of his nose and got it all over me!" screeches another. And of course, the most popular: "Mommy, I need more money!" Then, when one child calls out, "Mommy, I have to throw up!" you've got pretty much everything you need, so you can turn off the recorder and go home.

Keep the tape and the recorder in a drawer near your phone. Then, when you receive a call from a friend who wants to have a nice, quiet, adult conversation about the latest art film, or to review a recent concert, or just to talk about the vagaries of life, take the recorder from the drawer. Then, with the telephone pressed to one ear, insert the recorder's earpiece into your other ear and crank up the volume from the pizza place. Now, try to carry on intelligent conversation with your friend while a child's voice booms, "Mommy! Mommy! Look what I can do!" Voila! You have a taste of what it's like to be a mother.

A second suggestion to approximate what lies ahead once you join the wonderful sorority of motherhood is for you to go to your local fast-food restaurant and rummage through the trash cans for discarded food wrappers and bags. (Note: For obvious reasons, you should do this very late at night, very early in the morning, or in a neighborhood very far away from yours.) It's important that you find at least three bags that contain a fair amount of half-eaten, discarded food. (Day-old french fries soaked in catsup and remnants of bean and cheese burritos are premium finds.) Then return to the pristine car that you clean inside and out every Saturday morning and spread the contents of the food bags throughout the vehicle, making sure to get the greasiest and most odiferous food items into nooks and crannies that would seem to be impenetrable.

Then, if you've been lucky enough to find a packet of any condiment (mustard is fine, but mayonnaise is far and away the best), open the packet and rub its contents all over your hand. Then press your fingers against every possible inch of window space and chrome accessory. Finally, the most important part: When you drive off, be sure to turn on the heater to "high" and leave it blasting for the next two weeks, allowing the aroma of greasy and aging food to permeate your floor mats, seats, and roof liner.

These are just a few glimpses into the joys of motherhood. But don't get the wrong idea; it's not all fun and games.

TWO

ONE FINE DAY

"Choosing to become pregnant is like choosing to row across the Atlantic to Paris all by yourself. In a bathtub. You've always dreamed of seeing Paris, and in preparation for your trip you've talked to other women who have made the journey. You start out in calm waters, rowing strongly and gliding though the silkiness with ease, which makes you question what those other women told you. "This isn't so difficult," you say to yourself; they must not be as strong as you.

Then, as you reach the halfway mark, the seas become rough and choppy and all of a sudden you feel someone else in the boat with you, which means that you have to row even stronger because now you're rowing for two. Your back begins to ache, your legs and arms throb. And if this weren't enough, you begin taking on water. Lots of it.

But you row on, determined to experience the beauty of Paris; but you've been at sea for eight months and begin to question why you undertook such a long and exhausting endeavor. You wonder if it is worth it.

Then, just when you think you can go no farther, you see lights glowing in the distance. Paris! You will be there soon! You are so overcome by a feeling inside you that you begin screaming, partly out of joy and partly because of all the exhaustion you've been through. You row harder than you've ever rowed before, closing your eyes and screaming louder and louder all the while.

Then, suddenly, there is calm. You open your eyes and you are in a beautiful and peaceful park on the Champs d'Elysee. And as you take in every wonderful feature of the city, you realize that the journey was well worth the effort. Paris is absolutely more beautiful than you could ever have imagined. And as you caress the city, making it a part of you, you know that your life will never be the same.

—*Grandma Carol, Los Angeles, California*

★   ★   ★   ★   ★

It's about 5:15 P.M., and as you drive home from school in your hybrid, that strange new sensation comes over you again. You feel a bit lightheaded and dizzy, just like you felt when you were a little girl and your dad took you on your first spinning carnival ride. You also feel warm and notice a trace of perspiration forming on your upper lip. Your mom just went through menopause, and she described the same feelings. But you're only twenty-eight, so you couldn't be going through "the change" yourself, although you guess anything's possible, considering that *Enquirer* story you scanned while waiting in the supermarket checkout line about the woman in Singapore who gave birth to triplets at the age of eighty-seven.

But you suspect otherwise, because you've been experiencing this weirdness for the past week; most recently earlier in the day when you were leading your kindergarten class in a rendition of "The Turkey in the Straw."

"Oh, there was a little chicken, and she wouldn't lay an egg," your group sang with the enthusiasm, pitch, and volume only attainable by five-year-olds.

That's when you felt just a little woozy; and when you sat in one of the tiny little kindergarten chairs—your knees touching your chest—you were glad you chose to wear slacks to work, and not that skirt that your husband says makes your legs look "awesome." You stayed seated until the children finished their song and the lunch bell rang. Then you hurried to the teachers lounge, but you couldn't eat much because your appetite's been a little bit squirrelly the past several days. But the two full glasses of water sure tasted great.

As you get closer to home, you can't help smiling as you try to wrap your brain around the possibility. Could it be? Well, you're period's later than it's ever been, and the truth is, you and your husband have talked about it a lot lately, and he was as excited about the prospect as you were. You both have good jobs, you've managed to save some money, and since you both have health insurance, the expense of having a child wouldn't turn you into paupers. And your house has enough room for one more. So what if you have to give up a home office?

You begin calculating back, and determine that it probably happened—if it happened—about thirty-six days ago. Then it hits you: your neighbor Jill's thirtieth birthday party. You recall every detail of the evening, especially slow dancing with your husband under the warm August moon in Jill's tiki-torched backyard. There was something incredibly romantic going on with you two that night, and you smile when you think back to how you gazed romantically into each other's eyes while Barrry Manilow sang "Weekend in New England."

Then he whispered something into your ear; you responded with a sexy nod, and before the song had ended, the two of you had hightailed it out Jill's side gate and were quickly headed home for some private time.

You got back to the party an hour or so later, just in time to sing "Happy Birthday," which was followed by a group plunge into the pool. You got home at 1:30 A.M., removed your soaking clothes, and immediately hopped into bed.

But not to sleep. Again.

Then, as you begin to consider names—maybe "Sara" for a girl, "Jake" if it's a boy—you realize you are getting seriously ahead of yourself.

So you pull into the local pharmacy, determined to get an answer right away. You select a home pregnancy test and head for the register, but then you turn around and grab a second one from the shelf. This is because you're a female and, unlike your male counterparts, you are able to plan for almost any eventuality. This is just one of the many reasons women are given the responsibility of bearing offspring; if males gave birth—and even though they had nine months of preparation—once the baby emerged, they'd be, "Well, looky here! Where're we gonna put him?"

The reason you bought *two* pregnancy tests is because you didn't want to get your husband's hopes up by telling him you *might* be pregnant, only to have it be a false alarm. You know he's excited about starting a family, but you also know that he doesn't handle disappointment well, even though he's a lifelong Chicago Cubs fan. So your plan is to take the first test as soon as you get home; if it's negative, sure, you'll be a bit disappointed, but at least it's only disappointment for one, and you won't mention a thing. But if the first test is *positive*, and after you get done screaming your lungs out, you can collect yourself and calmly call your husband at work to make sure he'll be home at the regular time for dinner. Then later, when you tell him you *think* you might be pregnant, he'll insist on accompanying you into the bathroom while you take the test. And since you already know the result, the only dodgy part of this scenario will be for you to act as excited as you were a few hours earlier. But that should be no problem, because we have known how to fool men about their level of excitement for centuries.

So you go into your bathroom with the pregnancy test. It's the first time you've ever used one, and the difficulty of hitting the target makes you think that these devices were likely created by men, for whom urinating on a stick is not only easy, but probably has the potential to become their next big drinking game. But hitting the spot is not so easy for a woman, unless she's a yoga instructor or has a neck like E.T.

But eventually you get it right. And then you see the results.

For the next two hours before your husband arrives home, you will alternate between loony laughter and thankful tears as you set the table with the china and crystal goblets you received as a wedding present four years ago, and that you only use for very special occasions.

Then you begin to prepare his favorite meal—fettuccine carbonara—for which, of course, you are required to use the recipe that his mother thrust upon you at your engagement party. While the water boils and the sauce bubbles, you round up some wrapping paper and ribbon so the gift you have for him will look just perfect when you present it to him after dinner.

With everything right on schedule, you still have time to put on your sexiest dress—the one your husband's mother told you "shows entirely too much cleavage. You're a married woman, now!" And as you slip it on, you realize that tonight might very well be the last time you'll be able wear this hot little number for awhile.

When your husband walks in fifteen minutes later, the lights are down low and you greet him with a hug and a long passionate kiss.

"Wow," he says after you separate. "What's the occasion?" he adds, looking around the candlelit room. You can tell that he's mentally scrambling for some important date that's slipped his mind.

"Nothing special," you answer, knowing full well that your impish smile is saying otherwise.

"You look hot," he says, putting his arms around your waist and eyeing the low cut of your dress. "Are your boobs getting bigger?" he asks playfully.

He noticed it, too, you think to yourself. You thought you detected a slight change when you put on the dress, but chalked it up to your imagination.

"Oh, c'mon . . . How could that be?" you say dismissively, and he just shrugs. You're bursting to tell him the truth, but you have to stick to your plan: dinner and *then* his present. So you lead him to the dining table.

"Have a seat and I'll get the salad," you say, heading to the kitchen. As you go, you can feel his amorous eyes on you. You like that.

When you return with the salad, you see him uncorking a bottle of red wine; he pours himself a glass then moves to you.

"Wine, hon?"

"Sure," you say without thinking. You don't drink much, but what's an Italian dinner without red wine? Then, just as he's about to pour, you realize your mistake and cover your glass with your hand. "No!" you say. "No wine for me!"

Your husband eyes you curiously. "Are you all right?" he asks.

"I'm fine," you say, wondering how you can possibly keep the secret throughout dinner. He shrugs, and as you watch him dig into his salad, you smile. He is going to be such a great father. You observe him a while longer, then ask, "So how was your day? Anything exciting?"

"No. You?"

"Okay, you caught me," you blurt, caving. "I guess there's just no surprising you!"

Then you reach under your chair and grab the brightly wrapped present. "Here," you say as you hand it to him. He's completely baffled.

"What's this for?" he asks, now certain that he's forgotten an important date.

"You'll see," you tell him as you feel the perspiration forming in your palms. "Go on, open it."

He begins unwrapping it methodically.

"Faster!" you urge.

Obliging, he tears away the paper to find himself holding an unopened home pregnancy test. He studies it momentarily, then looks up to see you smiling at him.

"Are you saying that you . . . " he stammers, stunned.

"Could be," you tell him. "Should we go see?"

"Hell yeah!" he shouts, leaping from his chair.

He hands you the test and you both head for the bathroom, but then he returns to the dining table and nervously slugs down what's left of his wine.

Three hours later, you're both lying in bed. When your husband saw the positive result, he picked you up and swung you around the bathroom; then he quickly but gently set you down, so as not to hurt his delicate, pregnant wife.

After he kissed you two or three thousand times, he ran out to call his folks. They were ecstatic, although his mother did opine that "it's about time."

Then you called your mom and the two of you alternated between laughing and crying for the next forty-five minutes. Then you called your dad, and he was equally thrilled. "I can't believe it; my little baby is gonna be a mommy herself," he kept saying.

While you were talking to your father, your husband was online, setting up a savings account for your child. Then he had two more celebratory glasses of red wine, toasting you with your mineral water.

Because of the wine, your husband is soon fast asleep. But you're not at all tired, and your mind is racing. What color to paint the baby's room? How long will you be able to work before taking maternity leave? Natural childbirth? Who should we ask to be godparents? As these and other questions buzz through your brain, you realize that—for the first time in days—you are absolutely starving. In all the excitement, you completely forgot to eat. So you get out of bed without waking your husband and go into the kitchen, where you eat two heaping bowls of pasta, which you wash down with some guava nectar.

Then, you turn off the kitchen light and head back to the bedroom. As you cross your moonlit house, you get an image of the little child who will soon be scooting about your hardwood floors. Then you think of the wonderful man asleep in the next room and ponder all the spectacular things you will soon be experiencing together. Then, seemingly out of nowhere, you feel tears running down your cheeks.

Congratulations. Your adventure in the bathtub boat has begun.

THREE

NINE MONTHS, ELEVEN DAYS, AND SEVEN "WHAT WAS I THINKING?" HOURS

But who's counting, right? As we've already said, the trip to motherhood can be long and arduous. Those of you who are already moms know this to be true; but for you moms-to-be, allow us to provide you with some guideposts to alert you to some things you're likely to encounter during your incredible journey.

During your first month or so of your pregnancy—the stage a young mom friend of ours calls the euphoric "I still can't believe it" phase—you'll notice that your family and friends seem to be more concerned about your well-being than you are. For example: Before you were pregnant, you and your mom spoke by phone two or three times per week. Now, it's daily . . . often more than once.

"How are you feeling, honey?" is the first question she'll ask.

"Fine, Mom," you say.

"Are you sure?"

"Yeah, I'm sure."

"No swollen feet yet? Sore back?"

"No, Mom. This whole pregnancy thing has been a piece of cake," you tell her. "In fact," you add, "it's so easy that I'm thinking four or five kids would be just perfect for us."

You notice a curious pause; this is your mother covering the phone and having a good laugh at your expense.

Now let's flash forward six months; you are well into your third trimester. It's been the hottest and muggiest August in years, and with the cumbersome pregnancy bra you've had to wear lately, you've got enough perspiration between your breasts to go scuba diving. Your mom calls—right on schedule.

"How are you doing, honey?

"Doing?" you snap at her. "Well, let's see . . . My feet are so swollen I need clown shoes. My back feels like I move pianos for a living. I've got more water in me than Lake Tahoe, I need a forklift just to get out of bed, my hair has all the luster of an oil slick, and my emotions go from happy to sad to scared-to-death all within two seconds! Other than that, Mom, I'm doing just fine. Thanks for asking."

As soon as you finish your screed, you'll feel horrible about it. "Sorry, Mom," you say.

"It's okay, sweetie," she says comfortingly. "It will all be better soon."

Then she offers to take you to lunch and you gladly accept. The two of you enjoy a lovely afternoon, and just being with your mom at that particular time magically changes what had been a disaster day into a very pleasant one. Several times during lunch you catch your mom smiling at you proudly, and you hope that you can be as great a mom as she.

Now we'll discuss some "husband" behavior you'll probably encounter during your pregnancy. First, you should recall how cute you thought it was when he called his parents to announce, "Mom, Dad we're pregnant!"

But once you're in your eighth month, and need to put Crisco on your door jambs just to slide out of a room, the "We're pregnant" that he continues to use will have lost every ounce of its charm. So it's completely acceptable for an irritable pregnant wife to gently point out to her husband that his saying "We're pregnant!" is like you saying, "We're having a vasectomy!"

If he doesn't get the message, you might also remind him that although he professes to love you more than anything or anyone in the universe, he is the one responsible for making you constantly irritable, nauseous, and having to buy all your clothes at a sumo wrestler's garage sale.

And although he's been incredibly patient and attentive—going out in the middle of the night to satisfy your food cravings or to replenish your supply of feminine hygiene products—you need to remind him that *he* is not pregnant. Because if he were pregnant would he be so in favor of having natural childbirth? Or would he be ordering up enough anesthesia to keep himself pain free until his new child begins driving?

So in place of "We're pregnant" ask him to use "We're expecting" or "We're having a baby" and he's sure to go along with it. One thing you may not be able to change, however, is your husband's habit of nodding to your stomach, then elbowing his buddy and chuckling proudly, his sense of macho accomplishment there for all to see.

You will also notice during your pregnancy that your husband will open every door for you and even carry your purse when asked. And though he does these things out of his undying love for you, there are several advantages your pregnancy may offer to him. For example, the next time you're at a party and your condition dictates that you drink nothing stronger than mineral water, check out your husband at the bar. "Heck yeah, I'll have another mojito!" he says to his buddies. "*She's* driving."

But overall, your husband has been absolutely amazing; he painted the baby's room all by himself, and in the exact color you wanted. It took him a full Saturday to do the job, but he didn't want you exposed to paint fumes so he treated you and your best friend to a day of pampering at a local spa.

He's taken time off from work to go to every doctor appointment with you, and as you entered your eighth month, he got himself a second cell phone, for which only you have the number. You know that you're to call if you need anything; or more importantly, if you begin labor pains while he's at work. And just last week, he packed his and hers overnight bags for the hospital and placed them right by the front door so the both of you can make a quick getaway.

Then—a few days later—you notice a third bag by the door. Curious, you open it and inside you find a brand new video camera. Hmmm, he never mentioned anything about that, so when he gets home you ask him about it.

"It's so we have a video of the birth," he says matter-of-factly.

You had never considered such a thing; and after you give it some thought, you tell him you're not crazy about the idea.

"C'mon, babe, what's the problem?" he asks innocently. You recall that this is the same man who, on the first day of your honeymoon in Hawaii, refused to let you take a snapshot of him in his swimsuit because he thought his legs were too white. And now he wants to film your uterus.

You must be firm.

"The problem," you say, trying to be patient, "is that I don't want a camera in there while I'm in labor."

"Why not?" he asks with a bit of petulance. "It's a perfectly natural thing. What are you ashamed of?"

"I'm not ashamed of anything," you say, flaring at the accusation. "We're going to have our hands full in the birthing room," you remind him. "I need to be able to concentrate on the beauty of becoming a mother. And I need you to concentrate on the beauty of becoming a father, not worrying about whether my crotch is in focus!"

He sighs and you see that he will accede to your wishes. No video camera during birth. (Note: It will probably make him feel better to know that we talked to a good number of couples who *did* videotape the birth of their child, and not one of them ever looked at the tape. We did hear of one instance of a child's birth tape being viewed later, but that was only by accident. It seems it was mistakenly slipped into the VCR by a thirteen-year-old babysitter expecting to see *The Princess Bride*. When she saw what the tape really contained, she threw up.)

But forbidding your husband from bringing a video camera into the delivery room probably won't stop him from using his cell phone to get the picture of you holding the baby immediately after birth, umbilical cord still intact.

"Smile!" he says to you only seconds after you've undergone the most demanding and amazing physical feat known to man. We've all seen photos like this: a haggard new mom, with pale cheeks and matted hair that looks like she just swam through an oil spill, propped up against some pillows, holding her newborn, and smiling dutifully for the occasion. But if we look at these photos more closely, we'd likely see that this smile is saying, "Okay, I smiled. Now get that camera out of my face, or I swear I will jump out of this bed right now and rip your lips off!"

But then, at long last, the big day will arrive and will make itself evident by the wonderfully amusing physiological phenomena known as contractions. You might not recognize them at first, because it's almost certain that you've never experienced the feeling these he-devils bring. Mothers have used a lot of different words to describe these intermittent pains, and none of these words are the least bit flattering. So if you begin experiencing pains that feel like someone is grabbing at your insides and trying to rip them out, odds are you have started your contractions.

Congratulations . . . You're in the home stretch. And when your baby arrives and you hold your precious one for the very first time, none of what went before will matter because you are looking at the most beautiful thing you've ever seen.

Paris doesn't even come close.

FOUR

DAY ONE: GETTING TO KNOW YOU

I don't know if today's women are tougher than those of previous generations, but moms like me—whose kids are older—usually had their babies in the hospital, where we were able to stay for a day or two for a little post-delivery R and R. But today's new moms seem to come home almost immediately after giving birth. I'm not sure this is the best course of action, because my two days of rest in the hospital were the last restful days I had until my youngest child moved out, an occasion we celebrated by immediately changing the locks and the home security code.

But one thing is certain: Whether you stay in a hospital for a day or two, or come home with an infant whose age is measured in hours rather than days, there is one Mom Rule of which you can be certain: You will be exhausted. And regardless of how many new-parent books you read during your pregnancy or how many mommy classes you attended, now you're dealing with the real thing, not a rubber doll that poops and pees when you press a button on its back. The only button your newborn comes equipped with is the "Waahhh!" button. And as much as you might think you're up to the task, the truth is, you need help getting adjusted, as well as getting some rest. You have plenty of years to play Super Mom later, when you have one child due at a soccer match, another at a tutoring session, and a third home with the flu. Right now, you need someone who knows what she's doing. And in 99 percent of those cases, that person is spelled M-O-M.

Case in point: Tina, a young new mom, has an absolutely terrific mother-in-law who also happens to be an ob-gyn nurse. She and Tina get along wonderfully, and they get to see each other at least twice a week, because Tina's mother-in-law lives less than a mile away. Tina's mother, on the other hand, is a rather driven advertising executive who lives a three-hour plane ride from her daughter. Tina's mother, not a warm and fuzzy type, couldn't make it out in time for the birth because she had a client pitch session that would have been difficult to postpone.

So who does Tina want to be there when she comes home with her newborn—her terrific ob-gyn mother-in-law or her can't-cancel-a-meeting mother? Her mom, of course. Why? Because when Tina was a little girl, her mom—no matter how busy she was—always made sure that whenever Tina was sick, she stayed home from work and took care of her, guaranteeing that Tina had plenty of sympathy and tender loving care. That's what good moms do. And when Tina's mom arrived and first laid eyes on her new, day-old grandson, this type-A businesswoman broke down crying. It was hard for her to believe that her little baby had a little baby herself.

If, for whatever reason, your mom is not available to guide you through things such as diaper changing, burping, or tending to your bloated, aching breasts, choose either your best mom-friend or your mother-in-law. And if you have trouble choosing, ask the one who's the best cook.

If you're the mom of the new father, don't be jealous . . . this is just the nature of things. Of course, if you're lucky enough to also have a daughter who's a mom, you already know all about this. Just be patient; as your son's mom, you'll certainly be called on often—and, as your grandchild gets older, sometimes more often than you'd prefer.

We've noticed a funny phenomenon that often happens the day a young mother brings her baby home from the hospital. When you pull your car into the driveway, notice that when your neighbors hurry over, they will say many of the same things about your new baby that they would say if you'd come home with a new car.

"Oh, what a beauty," says Ed, as he looks into your baby's bright blue eyes.

His wife, Helen, takes a deep whiff of your newly bathed and powdered child. "And there's nothing like the smell of a new one," she says.

And Beth, mother of a two-year-old, chimes in, "Oh, seeing yours makes me think that maybe it's time we have a new one, too."

These people are all sincere in their joy for you. But as your child gets older—particularly if it's a male child, he will learn to scream everything at the top of his lungs as well as to delight in making strange noises come from his body . . . noises that often result in extremely unpleasant odors. As with your older car that's also starting to make loud noises and emit odors, it's at around this age that your neighbors will cease being so enamored with him.

And now, a word or two about the "D" word. Discipline, like it or not, is an essential part of being a mother. And emotionally, it can also be one of the most difficult. I know a number of mothers who say, "I want to be my child's best friend." Here's a Mom Rule about that from Kathy Gilbert, forty-two, and the mother of twin teenage daughters: "Don't try to be your child's best friend; work at being their best *mother*. Hope that their best friend is a well-rounded classmate who gets straight As while working part time, and who also volunteers at a homeless shelter—which leaves her very little time for texting, MTV, or boys. But she figures there will be plenty of time for that later."

And although doling out punishment is never easy, nothing is more difficult and heart wrenching as the first time you are forced to do it. And this usually happens around the time your little angel is about eighteen months old, because before that, it's generally a child's innocent misunderstanding or misinterpretation of the rules that results in minor misbehavior. It's not premeditated. But at around a year and a half is when a child is able to make a conscious decision to be mischievous. And when it happens, you have no choice but to discipline the child, as difficult as it may be. Believe me . . . I know.

When my oldest was a baby, she was like the ideal child. She never whined at bedtime; she woke up laughing every morning; and she always gladly ate whatever we put in front of her. We were certain that somehow, we had created the perfect baby.

Then, one rainy, gee-I-wish-I-could-sleep-in Saturday morning, it happened. My husband had worked an amazing amount of hours that week, so before we fell asleep Friday night, I volunteered to get up with our eighteen-month-old daughter.

The next morning at seven, I awoke to hear her gurgling happily in her room. I walked in to find her as I found her every morning, standing up in her crib, bouncing up and down in a kind of goofy semi-dance that only children and husbands at wedding receptions can do. And as always, she wore an ear-to-ear smile, and her hair was sticking out in every direction.

As was our routine, I lifted her sky-high from the crib and flew her, Tinkerbell-style, over to the changing table. And, as usual, she laughed that deep, uncontrollable laughter that is music to a mom's ears. Before long, she'd been changed and was in her high chair and I was serving her favorite breakfast, Cheerios with milk.

"Here you are, sweetie," I said, placing the bowl in front of her. That's when I saw something come over her face that

I'd never seen before: a look of utter disgust. And this look was not aimed at the Cheerios, but at me.

"My no why ti-ree-oh!" she said angrily.

"Of course you like Cheerios," I corrected.

"My no why ti-ree-oh!" she repeated. "My wuh pee-tah!" she said, pointing to the refrigerator where, inside, was the leftover pizza we'd ordered the night before.

"I know you want pizza, honey, but pizza is not for breakfast."

"My wuh pee-tah!" she screamed, looking at me with a level of disdain that I didn't expect to see from my daughter until she was at least thirteen.

"Eat your Cheerios. You cannot have pizza!" I said firmly.

As she stared at me with a sneer so evil and hateful that it would likely cause Hannibal Lecter to wet himself, she hoisted her bowl full of soggy Cheerios above her head.

"My wuh pee-tah!" she screeched one more time. Then she hurled the bowl, sending it careening off a cabinet and crashing to the floor.

I was stunned; I couldn't believe our sweet little baby could be so wicked. I looked at the cereal splattered everywhere, then back at her, expecting to see a face filled with remorse—a face that said, "I'm so sorry, Mom. I didn't mean it. Please forgive me, because I love you more than anything."

But instead I saw a challenging face that seemed to say, "So . . . what do you say to that, witch?"

I knew that she and I had arrived at our first showdown. Which of us would be the first to blink?

I decided that it wasn't going to be me, so I walked over and took her tiny, cereal-crusted hand and placed it firmly in mine. "You are a very bad girl," I said as I delivered a firm swat to my own hand as it was wrapped around hers.

I'm not sure if it was the sound of flesh smacking flesh, or the very idea that her mother could treat her like that, but my daughter's eyes got as big as pie tins as her bottom lip began to quiver. Then she let fly with the most agonized, betrayed wail I had ever heard. And soon, Hurricane Katrina had nothing on the tears streaming down her face.

Of course, I immediately felt horrible. What had I done? Would she ever find it in her heart to love me again?

Her screaming soon woke my husband, who stumbled groggily into the kitchen, his hair looking like I'd been sleeping with Lyle Lovett.

"What happened?" he mumbled in a froggy, morning voice.

"We had a little disagreement about breakfast," I explained.

"Oh, honey," he said tenderly as he lifted her from her high chair. "Did Mommy make you cry?"

Our daughter nodded, her crying ebbing into a series of staccato sobs.

"It's okay; Daddy's here now. Want to sit on my lap and eat breakfast with me?"

Our daughter nodded enthusiastically as he carried her to the refrigerator. Then he peered in, grabbed what he wanted, and for the next fifteen minutes, the two of them enjoyed a breakfast of orange juice and pizza.

Awhile later, I was still feeling guilty about our confrontation as I finished dressing. Then my daughter toddled into our bedroom and saw me checking myself out in the mirror.

"Mommy, doo boo-tee-foo," she said, looking up at me with big, loving eyes.

"Thank you, honey," I said, lifting her. "You are beautiful, too," I told her.

She giggled, then gave me a big whopping kiss on the lips. It was one of the nicest kisses I'd ever had—even though it tasted like pepperoni.

FIVE

HI-HO, HI-HO, IT'S BACK TO WORK YOU GO

Although everyone agrees that there's no such thing as a *non-working* mother, recent statistics indicate that 63 percent of mothers with young children work outside the home, with this number increasing to 76 percent for mothers of school-aged children. And if you just had a child and also have a job to return to, it's likely that you never dreamed six weeks of maternity leave could pass so quickly. You spent the first ten days adjusting to the reality that twenty-seven years of sleeping at least eight hours every night are a thing of the past. That's ancient history, just like your freedom to travel at a moment's notice, your plan to buy that spiffy little two-seater convertible, and going more than six hours without using the word "poo-poo."

But soon you find yourself thinking about returning to work, and because you've learned to appreciate the little chunks of sleep you're able to grab during the day at home, you wonder if it would be out of line to ask for your office to be equipped with a day bed and an apothecary of potpourri that smells like baby powder.

At about the four-week mark, you become very conflicted. The joy of being a mom is so beyond what you ever dreamed of, and you cherish the time you're able to spend with your newborn. But at the same time, you're beginning to miss the challenge and stimulation of your job, as well as the people you work with. In truth, you're kind of anxious to get back into the action. This makes you wonder if you're a bad mom.

Mom Rule: Get that thought out of your head. Moms hold jobs away from home for one of two reasons: They *want* to, or they *have* to. (Note: Recent studies indicate that only 4.5 percent of American workers actually like their jobs.) And it doesn't matter which group you belong to— love your job or otherwise—because as a new mom you've learned that caring for a newborn 24/7 is not an easy assign- ment. So looking forward to some adult conversation with people you like is completely normal.

But there are some tasks you'll need to attend to before you waltz back into your office after six weeks, loaded down with a new attaché big enough to hold all the baby pictures you brought to decorate your office. And one of these tasks—and certainly the most important—is setting up day care for your precious new baby.

A lucky few of you may have a husband or partner who works from home and can care for your child most of the time. Others of you may be blessed with two or more sets of grandparents who live locally and who are willing to share what you consider the joy and privilege of babysitting your uniquely gifted baby.

But because the average age for becoming a grandparent today is only forty-seven, many grandmas and grandpas aren't available to provide childcare because they're still working themselves or going off to Cancun with very little clothing because their youngest child—you—are out of the house. What all this means is that new parents have to find trustworthy commercial day care for their child; and anyone who has tried that recently knows how difficult that can be.

There are two primary resources for infant childcare: In-home care (where you take your child to a care provider's home) and preschools.

Be assured that most in-home childcare facilities are clean, well run, and nurturing. But there are some that don't quite measure up to their claims. Here are a few red flags that may indicate that a place is not quite what you're looking for.

You and your husband have made a noon appointment to visit Auntie Annie's Kiddie Haven, an in-home childcare facility you saw advertised in your local newspaper.

You show up a few minutes before noon and are pleased with the tidy house on a quiet, tree-lined street. You knock on the front door and a sixteen-year-old girl answers. She's on her cell phone.

"Is Auntie Annie here? We're the Smiths."

"You're early," she says, miffed at the interruption. "Mom'll be back in a minute. She ran out of wine."

You should also avoid any place that boasts "a completely fenced-in yard," only to find that the "fence" consists of yellow police tape.

And finally, you should look askance on any day care provider whose curbside mailbox is riddled with bullet holes.

On the other end of the childcare spectrum are "preschools" that accept children usually around the age of three, along with "pre-preschools," which often take children as young as six months.

Based on the experiences of my youngest daughter, Mischon, and her husband, Kevin, who "jumped through hoops" to get their daughter—and my youngest granddaughter—into a well-regarded pre-preschool near their home in Northern California, here's what you might have to look forward to:

1. Fill out an application. ($100 fee, non-refundable.)
2. Interview (with baby). Remember, this is only if your application passes muster. Then, depending on the strength of your application and interview, your child can be: A) accepted; B) rejected; or C) put on a wait list. It is recommended that you apply to several pre-schools in case your number-one school doesn't pan out, then you can shoot for your number-two choice. Remember, this is for pre-preschool, not Harvard or Yale.
3. Bite your nails while you wait. A week, two weeks . . . not a word. Then one day, a piece of mail finally arrives from the school. You open the envelope nervously, and as you unfold the letter, you are stunned by what it says. Was she accepted? Nope. Was she rejected? Nope. Wait listed? Nope. There is absolutely no hint as to the outcome, and not even a hint that you actually applied. Instead, it's a form letter addressed to "Friends and Parents of (name of preschool)." There is also a book of raffle tickets, which the letter encourages you to buy for $100, with the proceeds going to the school's enrichment fund. As you think about this, you realize that this is an out-and-out case of bribery. Does this school really expect you to send them a check for $100 before you know whether your daughter is even accepted there? How could they be so foolish?
4. A week later, you receive a letter informing you your child has been accepted. You heave a huge sigh of relief. Now that you're in their pre-preschool, it means you have a priority for their preschool, which begins at age three. It's now that you think back to that book of raffle tickets and pat yourself on the back for not

sending them a check for $100. Instead, you sent them a check for $200 and asked for another book of tickets. You're learning.

And now, a final word about working moms versus stay-at-home moms. Apparently it's not uncommon for a bitter rivalry to form between moms who have to work and those who don't. Okay, perhaps it's only one side who's bitter, but the rivalry can be fueled by those stay-at-home moms who have their child in day care only so they can "free up" their time. My daughter has experienced this firsthand, and takes the rivalry one step further: "These stay-at-home moms show up at day care in tennis outfits with lattes and mochas for the other parents! How do you compete with that? I feel like showing up in the morning with five-dollar bills and saying, 'Sorry, but *I* have to be at work at seven. Hope the line at Starbucks doesn't take up too much of your *free time*'!"

Did I raise a great kid or what?

SIX

A ROMANTIC WEEKEND AWAY: YOU, HIM, AND TWO VIBRATING CELL PHONES

Okay, so your spectacularly gifted baby boy is now six months old, and he's certainly the brightest child his age in your Mommy and Me group. Well . . . except maybe for that Justin kid who can count to three in both English and Spanish. But what do you expect from a kid with such an obnoxious mom who, by the way, often introduces herself as "Doctor" just because she has several PhDs before the age of thirty?

Anyway, as much as you and your husband adore being around your little boy, you both know that it's high time for the two of you to get away for a weekend full of some long-overdue private time. But now that you're a mom, you'll find that "getting away" isn't as easy as it used to be. The days of getting a call on Thursday night and you saying, "Palm Springs for the weekend? I am so there" are so over.

With a little one in the equation, a simple two days away can sometimes take two months of planning. The primary question, of course, is who do you trust to watch your precious one while you and your husband are off acting like hormone-driven teenagers? The longest you've ever been away from your baby is while you're at work. But overnight? For two nights? Without you? Having a set of grandparents living nearby can make this decision easier. But in this case, more is not better because having *two* sets of local grandparents can complicate things. Why? Because whatever set of grandparents you *don't* ask to look after your precious one will likely be crushed by your lack of confidence in them.

So what to do? And c'mon, admit it . . . You know that there's one set of grandparents that you'd feel better about watching your baby. So how do you go about it without hurting the other grandparents' feelings?

Try this: Ask your second choice if they have any travel plans coming up.

"As a matter of fact we do," they say. "We're going on a golf/spa weekend the fifteenth of next month."

And there you have it. Your decision is made for you. First, check with your preferred grandparents to make sure they're available, then make your getaway plans for the same weekend. The important part is not to tell Grandparents #2 until a day or two before; if they say they'll cancel their weekend to watch their beloved grandchild, you simply say that the plans have already been made, and you can't disappoint Grandparents #1. Then, to make Grandparents #2 feel better, say that of course you would have asked them to watch the baby in the first place if they hadn't had a trip planned.

If however, you don't have grandparents living nearby, your choices are limited to A) Your good friends Ron and Peggy, who are your baby's godparents and who love your child like their own . . . if they had their own. But they don't, because they don't want kids for another ten years; they want to travel . . . and party; and B) Asking one set of grandparents to come into town to watch the baby while you're gone. In this scenario, you are limited to the grandparents who live nearest you, favorite or not. It would beg too many questions if, say, you live in Oregon and you ask the favorite grandparents, who live in Florida, in favor of the other grandparents, who live south of Seattle. But whomever you go with, you still have lots to do, even if you've secured the services of Grandparents #1.

First, you'll probably make a detailed list on how to handle a baby, in case they've forgotten. Sure, they're only in their early fifties, but lately you've noticed your dad saying things like, "Where did I put my hat?" and saying to your mom, "How you doin', sunshine?" and then patting her on the rear—in front of people! He never did that when you lived at home.

I'll show you what I mean about lists. Awhile back, my daughter called to ask if I could watch my granddaughter, Claire, for four days while her childcare provider was away. Now mind you, I'm the mother to two grown daughters; Claire was six months old at the time.

When I arrived, I was greeted with two full pages of neatly printed notes, just in case—at my age—I'd forgotten which end the diaper goes on. Here are some excerpts:

At breakfast time, be sure to use high chair and bib. Really? Gee, I'd planned to sit her on the floor and put a mop to her after she was done.

After buckling her in, attach tray. Could you please be more specific? How do I attach it? With a belt? Scotch tape?

If she doesn't choose to eat her cereal by hand, it's okay to feed her with a spoon. No way! The little brat either eats with her fingers or she starves!

And finally: *When you change her on the diaper table, be careful she doesn't fall off.* What are you raising, a sissy? A few hard knocks will prepare her for life. Besides, the floors are carpeted.

And that's when I watched the baby at *their* house. If you're going to drop your baby off at a grandparent's house, you'll also need a list of what your baby eats, how often she eats it, her nap time, her bedtime, and her wake-up time.

You'll also list what the grandparents are allowed to do with her, and what they aren't. For example, if your child stays with your parents, and they live near the beach or a lake, you might forbid them to take your little daughter there for fear of sunburn, sand fleas, or whatever. But as a grandparent myself, let me warn you about something: All you have to do is tell grandparents what not to do and that is all the motivation they need to do it. Of course they will take their beautiful six-month-old grandson to the beach, just like they took you when you were six months old. How else will they show him off? But rest assured, your child will be surrounded by more umbrellas than a Seattle bus stop, be slathered with SPF 10,000, and drenched in enough bug spray to protect a troupe of Florida Boy Scouts.

You will bring all sorts of gear the grandparents will need to survive the forty-eight hours: car seat, stroller, portable bathtub, two diaper bags, and portable restraining bed rails that they can anchor between the mattresses of the double bed in the room directly across the hall from theirs.

Your parents will only use the car seat and the contents of the diaper bag.

You give your parents both your cell numbers, the number of the hotel, as well as of the restaurants you'll be having dinner each night. But they don't call one time; but that's okay, because you call them every few hours or so.

You and your husband are having a romantic dinner your first night away. When he excuses himself for the men's room, you check your watch: 8:30 P.M. Your son's bedtime was 8:00 P.M., so you take out your cell phone and dial. Your mother answers. "Hi, Mom. How's it going?"

"Super," your mother answers. "He's an absolute angel."

"He went to sleep without a problem?"

"Of course," your mother answers, gesturing "shhhhh" to your father, who's in the next room, tossing your six-month-old in the air and catching him on the way down. The baby is laughing uncontrollably, and in three more tosses, he will spit up in grandpa's shirt pocket.

You and your husband will have the most romantic, uninterrupted evening dinner you've had since your seventh month of pregnancy, all because of your parents taking care of your child just as you would.

Your son stays up till ten and goes to bed—snuggled in between Grandma and Grandpa—at 10:15 P.M.

When you pick him up late Sunday afternoon, he has just had a bath (in the kitchen sink), gone for a walk (grandma and grandpa switched off carrying him), and is dressed in brand new jeans and T-shirt (one of the seven new outfits they bought him). When you get home at 7:30 P.M., your son yawns and seems to be thrilled to get to bed a little earlier than usual.

After you put him down, you and your husband snuggle on the couch, enjoying a glass of wine and recounting all the wonderful things of your first weekend away in ages. You're both thrilled that things went so well with the grandparents, who seemingly followed every one of your instructions to the letter.

Soon, you both go to bed and fall into a blissful sleep, cuddling in each other's arms.

The next morning, as you scurry to get everything ready to take your son to day care, you wonder how all that sand got in his diaper bag.

SEVEN

XX/XY: A SYMBOL PLAN

When a child is first born, its gender is usually the first thing new parents check. For those parents who know if they're having a son or a daughter way ahead of time, the first thing they check is their baby's number of fingers, toes, amount of hair, and resemblance to Mom or Dad. For those who don't choose to know their child's gender before birth, it's not unusual for an expectant dad to say, "We don't care what it is," although 50.5 percent of him hopes for a boy "to carry on the family name," even if the family name is something like "Dummtzhit."

"Jack and Jane Dummtzhit announce the birth of their child, Dickie Dummtzhit!" Maybe some names need not be carried on as much as others.

In any event, the new dad will get over the minor disappointment of not having a son as soon as he holds his daughter for the first time. And when she manages to stare up at him with her pure dark brown eyes, Dad's first thought will be, *She is absolutely gorgeous.* His second thought, which follows very quickly, will be, *Boy? What boy?*

And thus will begin a lifelong father/daughter friendship and love affair. And as this little girl's mom, you will also have a lifelong relationship with her. But don't be surprised if sometimes along the way, most likely in her teens, this relationship takes a couple of years off for bad behavior.

This is all based in basic biology that we'll try to explain simply. The chromosomes that make a female a female are XX. The male chromosomes are XY; the significance of this will become evident as your child moves through life. In a young girl's early years, the chromosomal structure has no real relevance or meaning. But when she gets to "that age"—you know, the same age you were when you thought your mother was an absolute shrew who couldn't be tamed—this is the time that a daughter's XX begins engaging in hand-to-hand combat with a mom's XX; and there's no winning when four Xs come together because it's one X too many—even for something as simple as tic-tac-toe.

But with your son, you will only have three Xs between you, which is perfect for any party game.

Below you'll find some chronological probabilities that will help you navigate the ebbs and flows of a mom's relationship with her son versus her daughter, as each moves toward the ultimate goals: adulthood and apartments elsewhere.

BIRTH TO 3 YEARS

These years are, from a mom's point of view, pretty much gender non-specific. Son or daughter, you will regard your child as the cutest, most intelligent, and best-behaved toddler in the world. You will cuddle and coddle either gender equally, and dress them in cute clothes, which they will be proud to wear. Your husband will also exhibit very little gender distinction, although—as a male child nears the age of three—your spouse may begin to introduce him to the hilarity of making odd sounds come from the male body.

3 YEARS TO 7 YEARS

It's within these years that the differences between a son and daughter begin evidencing themselves. In the area of clothing, your daughter still likes to "dress up" and wear whatever Mommy wears, and loves new dresses and outfits. Your son, on the other hand, begins to "dress down" and wear what his dad wears. And, again like his father, he will chafe when you make him dress up for an occasion he considers unimportant, like going out to dinner or visiting his grandparents.

For daughters, these are usually the years when they begin to show their natural nurturing instincts, and begin playing with dolls. For sons, these years are spent tearing the arms off their sisters' dolls. And whacking each other with plastic baseball bats. But strangely, this is when a mom—since she was never a boy—becomes fascinated with young male behavior, and will begin to see some charm in it. Also, she will often fiercely defend her son's behavior to the mothers of less adorable boys. Likewise, this is when a dad—to whom young female behavior is a mystery—begins to see the beauty in his daughter's ability to "play pretend." This is why you will often see a father sitting in his favorite chair watching a ball game while his five-year-old daughter plays "beauty shop" and has his hair soaked and tied into corn rows held together with bread ties. During these pretend times, a dad quickly learns that he is not allowed to call his daughter by her given name, but must call her "Sandy," the owner of the beauty shop. Nor does his daughter call him "Daddy" in her beauty parlor. Instead, he is given a name that holds much more romance for a young girl—like Zack or Cody or the first name of any Disney Channel star.

It is also during this age period that a mother will first refer to her son as "Mommy's big boy"; and when a father might call his daughter "Daddy's little girl." Make note of this: you will see its importance soon.

7 TO 11 YEARS

Moms: If you have a daughter, these years are when you will see her begin to change from a *little* girl into a *young* girl. She will gradually lose interest in dolls and fantasy, which will be replaced by a blossoming interest in boys and clothes. These four years are Mother Nature's way of giving you a head's up on what lies just around the corner.

For boys, there is very little emotional development that goes on during this period. They will continue doing the same things they've been doing, except louder, dirtier, and smellier. But there is one thing that usually enters early on in the lives of children of both genders in this age range: sports.

Young boys have been participating in sports for centuries, and it wasn't all that long ago that it was "boys only" territory. But with the long-overdue adopting of legislation like the NCAA's Proposition 48, which mandated that colleges and universities expand their women's athletic programs to near parity to those afforded men, young girls are now able and encouraged to participate in sports—both team or individual. And where girls of a generation ago only had a few, if any, female sports stars to emulate, girls today can shoot for the same athletic goals as Mia Hamm, Brandi Chastain, Annika Sorenstam, Jenny Finch, Cheryl Miller, Picabo Street, and hundreds of other young women who are not only successful in athletics, but also in life (and many of whom who are now mothers as well).

Gone are the days of little girls' activities being limited to ballet, scouting, and gymnastics—all of which, by the way, continue to remain extremely worthwhile pursuits.

We mention this because the youth sports boom has not only impacted girls everywhere, but it has also allowed a father to take a more hands-on role in his daughter's activities. I guarantee you that, twenty-five years ago, you would never, ever, have heard a dad say to one of his buddies, "Gee, Stan, I'd love to play poker tonight, but I want to go to my daughter's Girl Scout meeting and see how those cookie sales are going." Or, "Golf Saturday? No can do. My nine-year-old has a ballet recital coming up and I need to work with her on her pliés and her fourth arabesques."

But today, at girls' softball, soccer, basketball, volleyball, and even lacrosse games, you see proud moms and dads cheering from the grandstands, or passionately coaching on the sidelines. And this is a very good thing, as is anything that brings parents and children together. But there's also an advantage for moms as well. Recently, we were at a large sports complex where there must have been twenty or so soccer fields in full use by teams made up of kids of all ages, from four-year-old boys to sixteen-year-old girls. We were there to see our favorite nine-year-old neighbor play. And although his game was really exciting and tied with little time left, we noticed that his mother would often check her watch nervously and occasionally scan the parking lot. During a timeout, we asked what was going on, and she told us that her eleven-year-old daughter had a game in fifteen minutes and hadn't yet arrived. No sooner were these words out of her mouth than her husband's car wheeled into the lot. Out of the front seat jumped their daughter, dressed in her Girl Scout uniform. As she scurried into the backseat, her father got out, closed the door, and stood sentry for what seemed like only a few seconds, until the back door opened and the girl bounded out, wearing her soccer uniform and trying to put on her shin pads as she sprinted to join her teammates.

As the father approached us, we smiled at the T-shirt he wore with unabashed pride.

It read: SOCCER DAD.

So, moms, not only do sports bring dads and daughters even closer, but they also finally give your husband just a small taste of the schlepping you've been doing for years.

EIGHT

THE TWEEN AND TEEN YEARS: MAKING CHARDONNAY YOUR FRIEND

Okay, Mom, we told you earlier that if you have a daughter, you should be expecting big changes. Now that she's sashaying into her teens, you might want to fasten your seatbelt, because there will be times that you will want to jump out of your chair and strangle that "younger you" sitting across the table; the one who is rolling her eyes and spouting things like, "I wish you never had me!" This would also be a good time to lower your oxygen mask, because yelling and screaming will require a lot of your breath.

Let's use fashion as an example: Where just a few years ago she wanted to dress like mommy, now she wants to dress like Mimi, the really popular and prematurely mature fourteen-year-old who goes to her middle school and dates a guy in a band.

Disappearing are the days of mother and daughter agreeing on the same outfit. During this period, your daughter's reaction to clothes you buy for her will progress from, "Mom, can we take it back and try a new store for a change?" to "I'm not wearing that!" to "Are you kidding? Why didn't you just buy me something that says 'Dork' on the back?" You will also see that her "pretend" days of

putting on lipstick and mascara are over; she's no longer pretending.

When you talk to your husband about this, he says he "thinks it's cute; she's just growing up. What's the harm of that?" When you hear this, you pray that he's double jointed, because in a few short years, he'll want to kick himself in the rear for even thinking such a thought.

If you have a son, things will be quite different. First, he's becoming increasingly easy to shop for: funky shorts, sneakers, and T-shirts with images of anything to do with sports or music. And as long as the brand new things you buy him don't *look* brand new, you're good to go. And should you buy him something that he doesn't particularly like, he probably won't say anything because he, unlike a daughter, cares about your feelings. "Thanks, Mom, it's really cool," he'll tell you politely. You'll only learn that it wasn't so cool when you pack him up for college years later and you find it stuck in the bottom of a drawer, folded exactly the way it was when it left the store.

Personal experience, as well as input from scores of mothers of teenage daughters, indicates that the most trying years in the mother/daughter relationship are between the ages of fourteen and eighteen. Not at all coincidentally, this is when your daughter's XX chromosomes are kicking her hormones into overdrive, while your XX-based hormones are . . . well, who knows what they're doing? What all this means is that girls of this age begin their full-speed-ahead voyage into womanhood—both physiologically and emotionally. And, because your daughter sees you as un-hip and ancient, it's a voyage she assumes A) You've never taken; or B) If you *have* taken it, it was so long ago that you've lost the road map.

There will likely be ongoing conflict in virtually every area of discussion, including, but not limited to: dating, dress, curfew, dating, hairstyle, hair color, dating, obedience, respect, academics, bedroom cleanliness, dating, music, R-rated movies, cleavage, tattooing, choice of friends, and dating. Add to those all the specific Mom Rules each mother has for her teenage daughter and you can see the possibility of real friction. Here are just a few from my daughter, Dionn, who is finally experiencing the joy of having a teenage daughter on her hands:

- "No riding with boys, even if it's just for a few blocks."
- "No going to a movie with a boy I haven't met face-to-face. And this does not mean Facebook-to-Facebook!"
- "No texting at the dinner table."

Every topic, no matter how harmless, has the possibility of exploding into an all-out war. Try this one on for size:

It's noon on a Saturday, and after doing laundry, taking the dog to the vet, and sitting through your youngest's tee-ball game, you have finally found some time to peruse the morning paper. Your seventeen-year-old daughter has just pulled herself out of bed and is sprawled on the sofa, wearing pajama bottoms and a T-shirt, and slurping from a bowl of cereal that she has perched on her chest while she texts maniacally. Your instinct is to tell her to sit up straight, not to text while she's eating, and after she finishes her breakfast, to get in and clean her room enough to see if that Little Mermaid carpet she begged for when she was six still exists under her pile of clothes and teen magazines.

But you are enjoying the current silence—no matter how uneasy—between you two, so you decide to skip all that for now. You turn the page and an advertisement catches your eye.

"Hmmm, Macy's is having a big sale this weekend," you say to yourself innocently.

"Who cares? You're not dragging me down there," she says, not bothering to look up from her phone.

"Who said anything about *dragging* you anywhere?" you ask.

"I could tell by your voice," she says. "You think I should dress all lacy-Macy's," she sneers.

"And what's wrong with Macy's?" you say before you can keep the words from spilling out of your mouth, knowing that your question will undoubtedly receive a vituperative, smart-mouthed reply.

"Nothing. If you're a geek loser—or *your* age." Then, after a slurp of cereal, she adds, "I don't know why you won't let me shop at Sugar 'n' Spice."

You feel your temperature rising. You want to avoid an argument, but you just can't let some things go, so you decide to answer: "Well, number one: Sugar 'n' Spice is too expensive. And number two: You are not a prostitute."

Okay, so you took the gloves off. Let the bout begin. And we know where it will end: She will accuse *you* of accusing *her* of promiscuity and loose behavior just because she went to a movie with a boy named Troy, whom you overheard boasting lasciviously to one of his jock friends in the high school parking lot that "when girls think *Troy* they think *Trojan*s!"

The accusations continue to fly and will likely end with your daughter stomping off to her room screaming, "I will be so glad when I get out of here and go to college!"

But before she can slam her door, you make sure you have the last word, even if it's misplaced. Although she works hard in school and gets very good grades, you add, "College? If you don't start cracking your books, you'll be lucky to get into traffic school!"

And so, this is how "the four or five years from hell" are likely to go.

On the other hand, your daughter and her father will get along famously during these times. He will be the mediator between the two of you, usually siding with her and cajoling you into retracting your latest grounding, or relaxing what he considers your Elizabethan curfew rules. Of course, he will always tease her by threatening to grill every male suitor that comes a-calling, but she takes this as flattery, knowing that her big, strong dad is just looking out for her. It is also your husband who will have the bravery and patience to teach her to drive and who will never miss an opportunity to tell her how smart and beautiful she is.

Now, quickly, let's look at the same Saturday scenario, but this time you're dealing with your seventeen-year-old son. As you peruse the paper at noon, he, too, has just gotten out of bed and sits at the counter in T-shirt and gym shorts, slurping cereal, reading the Sports Page, and scratching himself.

"Hmmm, Macy's is having a big sale this weekend," you say to yourself.

"Yeah?" he says, looking up from the paper. "If you're going, would you mind picking me up some medium boxers and size-10 gym socks?"

"Be happy to. Any special brand?"

"Hey, whatever you always get me is perfect." Then he gets up, dumps his cereal bowl in the sink, and gives you a big kiss on the cheek. "Thanks, Mom," he adds. Then, as he heads off, he thinks of something else. "Mom, you know that dress shirt Dad bought me to wear with my sport coat?

Do you think you could exchange it for something a little less . . . Ryan Seacrest-y?"

"Sure," you laugh. "Anything specific?"

"Whatever you think is cool."

Then he sprints toward the bathroom, sports page folded under his arm.

See? XX/XY . . .

But take heart, Mom, the treacherous daughter waters will gradually grow calm. This usually happens when she does move off to college, or when she gets a job and moves into an apartment with a girlfriend. Nothing like a little distance and absence to help you get to know each other better.

And when she meets her soul mate and announces that she will soon become a wife, she will likely seek and accept your advice in nearly every aspect of her wedding planning.

And on that magical day, when she walks down the aisle in the gown that she asked you—and only you—to help her pick out, you will be overcome with motherly pride at the beautiful, self-confident, and educated woman that your strong-willed teenage girl has become.

Then, while she and your beaming husband approach the minister, arm-in-arm, you can't help smiling at a memory that just then pops into your head: When your daughter announced her engagement, the first place she registered was Macy's.

NINE

CREATIVE MOMS: PUTTING THE "D-I-S" IN "D-I-S-C-I-P-L-I-N-E"

The disciplining of one's children goes all the way back to the dawn of time when Cain had that little contretemps with Abel . . . or was it the other way around? Either way, Cain was kicked out of paradise to spend the rest of his life as a lonely man. This is not unlike my cousin Randy, who was finally kicked out of the house by my aunt when, on his sixty-third birthday, he extinguished his birthday candles by systematically spitting on each one. Randy now lives his life as a lonely man in a dingy two-room apartment, although family rumor has it that he's recently made a female acquaintance he calls "Chi-Chi." But that's for another book.

Further evidence indicates that, over years, the job of disciplining has somehow fallen on the shoulders of moms, perhaps because the dads were out hunting, gathering, or looking for a really reasonable sushi bar. In fact, some of the earliest petroglyphs depict a cavewoman disciplining her cave-son by banishing him to a corner of a grotto, his face to the wall. The naughty boy was also made to wear what seems to be mankind's first version of a dunce cap, which was fashioned from an inverted mastodon tusk.

In the Middle Ages, when a child misbehaved, a mother would often force the offender to walk directly behind a team of recently fed oxen . . . barefooted. And during the American Revolution, when a youngster stepped out of line, he or she lost all after-school play privileges, and was immediately placed in mandatory fife lessons.

More modern methods of disciplining include grounding your child, banishment to his bedroom, revoking driving privileges, taking away a cell phone, and setting earlier curfews. And while many of these time-tested methods remain effective, one in particular has had its impact diminished by technology: sending your child to his/her bedroom. Although this may have been a very effective punishment twenty-five years ago, today a bedroom is exactly where your child—particularly your teenager—most wants to be. First and most importantly, it is away from you, and with a computer, television, and video games, what else does an adolescent need? Sentencing your teenager to three hours in her bedroom is like sentencing your husband to three hours at Hooters.

A mom learns that—the older her child gets—the more difficult it is to find disciplinary action that works . . . or that their aging children will take seriously, instead of responding with a facetious, "Yeah, Mom, right. That's a good one." Once children become relatively mature (a phenomenon that usually occurs in sixteen- to seventeen-year-old girls and thirty-year-old boys) they are very good at evaluating how serious you are about your threats, and how committed you are to enforcing them.

We're sure that most moms know every trick in the book. But let us mention one we've not heard from anyone else that comes from my sister-in-law, Jeri. It's a very simple drill she designed to enforce the curfew rules that she set for her three lovely, but strong-willed teenage girls.

Before any of her daughters would go out for the night, Jeri would be very specific about what time they needed to be home, and also warned them what their punishment would be if they were even a few minutes late. "I want you home by midnight, Sue, or you will not be going to that dance tomorrow night, understand?"

"Gotcha, Mom," her oldest daughter would nod.

Or maybe it was, "Carrie, if you're not home by 12:30 A.M., no beach tomorrow because you'll be home washing Dad's and my car, right?'

"Right, Mom," sighed her youngest.

And what did Jeri do to guarantee her children were home on time? Sit in a darkened living room, peering through an opening in her drapes, waiting for the appointed hour? Fight to stay awake in front of *The Tonight Show*? No. She and her husband would go to bed around 10:30 P.M. and be fast asleep by 11 P.M. But this was only *after* Jeri had set the alarm clock right next to her bed for the exact minute her daughter was to be home. The girls knew that if their mom's alarm clock sounded, it meant they weren't home in time to get in the front door, run upstairs, and disarm it. And that they were busted.

This method worked very well, and all throughout her daughters' teenage years, the alarm only went off a handful of times, most notably when middle daughter, Katie, found herself standing outside her front door with five minutes to spare. Unfortunately for the vivacious Ms. Kate, what she *didn't* have to spare was her house key, which she'd forgotten to take with her. She thought of ringing the doorbell, but because her dad's snoring could drown out a John Deere diesel, she feared her folks wouldn't hear it, meaning that her mom's alarm would go off while Katie was standing at the threshold of the Promised Land.

Thinking fast—but like many teenagers, not altogether clearly—Katie decided to remove a downstairs screen and climb in a window. And she would have made it in time, had she not forgotten her parents' new silent security system. She was able to remove the screen, but as she tried to force open the window, she heard tires screeching, and soon found herself bathed in the blinding ray of a white-hot spotlight.

"Hold it right there," came a voice from someone she couldn't make out, no matter how she squinted.

Eventually, Katie showed the security man her ID and got everything straightened out. By this time, her folks had been awakened, both by the commotion and by Jeri's blaring alarm clock.

The next afternoon, Katie found herself mowing the lawn instead of playing in a scheduled volleyball tournament, even though she pled her case, pointing out that the security company's report proved that she had begun removing the screen a full three minutes before her curfew time. Jeri listened thoughtfully and then rendered her ruling. "Sorry, Kate, but you know my Mom Rule: The alarm clock never lies."

★   ★   ★   ★   ★

And now, on to younger children, who are easier to discipline because A) They are much easier to intimidate because B) You are significantly larger than they are.

As a mom gains experience, she will learn what form of standard discipline works best on her pre-teen child. Smart moms swap trade secrets all the time, and soon compile notebooks full of effective discipline methods.

But for those of you who might be looking for something a little different, here are some pretty clever methods of discipline from a few of the moms we talked to.

Mary Binning of Orange County, California is the married mom of two kids: son Billy, age fourteen, and daughter Bernie, age thirteen.

Because Mary's Mom Rule #1 is: "Public shaming is an effective deterrent to bad behavior," she developed the Hester Prynne Method, which she employs—and highly recommends—for misbehaving children. Here's how it works:

Instructions: Take a three-inch notepad (similar to a Post-It note), and print a large, brightly colored letter on it. (Note: the letters will vary, depending on the misbehavior patterns of each individual child.) Here are some of most common letters Mary uses with her children:

- *"V" stands for "Victim." Used when whining or complaining.*
- *"T" stands for "Tattle Tale." Punishment for rat-finking on the other child. (Note: the other child must never be simultaneously punished, even though the intelligence gained from the tattler may come in handy at a later time.)*
- *"R" is for "Roughmouth." Punishment for crude, insulting language or otherwise repeating an expression Dad uses.*

Immediately upon observing your child's bad behavior, do not give a warning. If you do, this is bad behavior on your part and you must wear a large "W" (for "Warner," or perhaps "Wuss,") yourself. Rather, as soon as you witness the violation, you must immediately affix the appropriate "Scarlet Letter" on your child's shirt and remind him/her that everyone will see it. Hint: The prime location for the "Scarlet Letter" is on the back of the shirt, right next to the "Kick Me" sign. It's also wise to pin it on, rather than use a sticky Post-It, because this makes it more difficult—and possibly painful—to remove. Even if the child is simply in your home, there is a wonderful aura of shame in having to wear this sign of misbehavior. The length of time the "Scarlet Letter" should remain on the shirt is not important. I usually leave it on until the next offense, when it's time to change letters.

Note: For extra effect, keep a stack or two of "Scarlet Letters" placed about the house in locations readily visible to your children.

★　★　★　★　★

Here's another story about disciplining that comes to us from our friends Dave and Patti Coulter. It involves Dave's adult daughter, Shannon Goar, and an experience she had with her then preschool–aged daughter, and how Shannon taught the little one an important, universal Mom Rule: "Safety First!"

Here's how Patti tells it:

Shannon was driving her adorable, but precocious, four-year-old daughter, Lindsey, to preschool one morning. The sun was shining; the birds were singing; it had all the makings of another glorious Fort Worth day . . . until Shannon heard a loud click *come from the backseat.*

She turned to see that Lindsey had unbuckled the seat belt from her safety car seat. "Buckle it back up, sweetie," Mom instructed the toddler, to which the usually pleasant and agreeable Lindsey replied, "NO, I DON'T WANT TO!" Mom repeated her order, but only got defiant "NOs!" in return.

Her frustration mounting with each screech, Shannon pulled over to the curb, got out of the car, and buckled her daughter back into her car seat. Lindsey just stared at her mother sternly, but sat perfectly still in her seat as her mother got back behind the wheel.

Then, as she pulled away from the curb, snap, unbuckle, crackle, pop! *Off went the seatbelt again.*

Shannon's patience was quickly evaporating as she turned and used her best "angry mom" voice: "Put that back on right now!

And I mean it!" This was met with ear-piercing screams and Lindsey kicking the backseat so hard that it likely damaged the car's suspension. And the belt remained unbuckled.

Shannon had really had it by now, and wished she could make her four-year-old walk to preschool. Or better yet, to reform school. Once again, she pulled to the curb; but this time the guardian angel of all moms must have been looking down sympathetically, because as Shannon got out of the car, she noticed a motorcycle policeman parked just ahead. She approached him, at first thinking she should ask if he could possibly lock Lindsey up and throw away the key; but then her mother's sanity returned, so she simply explained the situation to the officer and asked if he could impress on her daughter the importance of keeping her seat belt buckled.

A few seconds later, the big imposing, uniformed figure approached the car and stuck his still-helmeted head in through the rear window. Lindsey's eyes grew to the size of saucers as he explained why she should obey her mother and always wear her safety seat belt. If she didn't, he said, he might have to get Santa Claus involved in all this. Or worse, cart Lindsey off to jail.

Snap, crackle, pop, buckle!

From that day forward, Lindsey never removed her seatbelt and always reminds her parents to buckle up should they forget.

Patti also suspects that, someday not too long from now, Lindsey will very likely brag to her friends, "My mom rules because she kept me out of jail!"

So be strong, moms. Although meting out the discipline is often difficult and painful, stay the course. Your kids will never be perfect, and neither will you. But be assured that once your kids pass through their confrontational years, they will appreciate how important it was for you to set boundaries for them . . . just as they will almost certainly do for their own kids.

TEN

IT'S A BIRD ... IT'S A PLANE ... IT'S SUPER MOM!

We've already looked at the statistics showing that the majority of young moms are employed outside of the home. But there is still a huge number of stay-at-home moms who work every bit as hard as their out-in-the-workplace sisters.

Throughout any given day, these moms are called upon to be caregivers, chauffeurs, nurses, cooks, laundry workers, educators, disciplinarians, and best friends. And in addition to all this, many stay-at-home moms also have part-time jobs that allow them to wrangle the kids and still contribute to the family income.

After getting input from a landscape of stay-at-home moms—and in many cases, from their husbands—about their daily responsibilities, we've created a composite that we think is representative of an average young family today.

We'll call them the Johnsons. The mom, Anna, and the dad, Bob, are both thirty-four. Their two children are daughter Chloe, age four and a half, and son Davey, eighteen months. Anna is home with the kids, but also spends at least four hours a day at her computer, working part-time for a medical billing company; Bob is a systems manager at a hip and thriving software development company. Chloe is in preschool three days a week. Davey is already on several waiting lists.

The Johnsons are busy, yet happy; they live in a three-bedroom house in a relatively new development located in the far suburbs, and Bob has a ninety-minute drive to work.

Here's a look at a typical day's schedule . . .

06:30   Bob leaves for work after kissing his sleeping wife and kids. He forgets to switch on the coffee pot, because he's preoccupied with something that weighs heavily on his mind: making his picks for the weekly office football pool. They're due today.

07:00   Anna gets up with Davey; she changes him, puts him in his high chair, and peels him a banana. Then she reaches for some hot coffee to get her day jump-started. Darn you, Bob!

She hurries in to wake Chloe, who's an amazingly heavy sleeper, and when Anna tries to jostle her awake, Chloe flails and accidentally overturns her fish bowl. Nemo and Tinkerbell, her goldfish, fall to the floor and slither under the bed. Hector, the family cat hurries in. Where the hell is that coffee?

07:55   Anna pulls into the "drop-off" lane at Chloe's preschool, which starts at 8:00. The line moves unusually slow, and there seems to be a bottleneck ahead. A lot of mothers are honking, and Anna joins them, because she has to be back home for an 8:15 conference call with her boss.

07:56   At Bob's work, he walks in and is greeted by the aroma of freshly brewed coffee wafting from his company's "bistro." He goes in to fetch a cup and sees that the young guy he hired last month once again brought in two dozen donuts and assorted pastries. What a suck-up! Bob selects a ham and cheese croissant.

08:06   Anna finally makes it to the front of the "drop-off" line and Chloe scurries out. Anna sees that the traffic snarl was caused by a first-timer dad who came in the wrong way, using the "pick-up" lane (open only from 2:45 to 3:30 daily) instead of the "drop-off" lane (open from 7:30 to 8:10 daily. Signs are posted everywhere, nimrod!) Not only is the poor man being berated by upset moms who will now be late for work, he's also receiving a "ticket" from the school's principal.

08:18   Anna pulls into her driveway with a screech. As she removes Davey from his car seat, she sees that he has soiled through his diaper. The car begins to assume an aroma of old bananas.

08:19   At work, Bob makes the important decision of selecting the Vikings over the Rams.

08:22   Anna finally logs onto her conference call. She has cleaned Davey's behind, but he's still bare-bummed as she carts him about while she listens on speaker phone to her boss explaining every detail of the new, improved billing form she created. Near the end of the conference call, Hector the cat wanders in and gags on the carpet, depositing what's left of the late Nemo and Tinkerbell.

09:00   Anna has dressed Davey and put him in his playpen, wiped up the goldfish, and is thinking about a shower as she finally sips her first cup of coffee. The doorbell rings; it's the cable man, and he's there to install the digital cable for the upgraded sports package Bob ordered. Shouldn't take more than an hour or two. Tops.

09:05   Bob goes for the Packers over the Bears. Then he goes for another croissant.

09:15   Anna has learned that the cable man's name is Clay, who is now sitting across the kitchen table from her. When she offered him a cup of coffee, she was just being polite and didn't expect him to accept. After fetching him cream and sugar (actually he requested a sugar substitute, saying, "I need to stay thin 'cause I gotta crawl under a lot of houses"). Anna peeks at the wall clock. It's time for Clay to get under the house and for her to get under a nice hot shower.

09:30   Aaaahhhh . . . Anna's finally beginning to feel human. Although Clay seems like a trustworthy fellow, Anna still took the precaution of hauling Davey and his playpen into her bedroom and locking the door while she showered and dressed. Refreshed, she tosses Davey onto the bed and begins to wrestle with him and he laughs uproariously. But soon their roughhousing is interrupted by Clay's faraway voice: "Mrs. Johnson, help!"

09:35   Anna finds herself kneeling in her backyard, peering into the dark crawlspace under her house, where Clay has managed to get himself hopelessly wedged between a four-by-eight support beam and the house's cement slab.

09:37   Jean-Michel, the chef employed at Bob's company so that employees aren't inconvenienced by always having to go out to eat, comes into Bob's office to take his lunch order. Bob orders a slab of ribs.

09:40   Anna offers to call 911, but Clay objects; he could be fired. So instead, Anna locates a long-handled outdoor broom, reaches under the house, and places the broom's head against the small of Clay's back. She pushes as hard as she can and, after a few grunts, Clay is freed.

Meanwhile, Davey, whom Anna let run around on their back lawn during all this, has decided to play in Hector's outside litter box.

10:15   Anna has once again cleaned Davey, and with him safely in his crib for his morning snooze, and Clay safely (please, God) under the house, Anna turns on her computer. There's work to be done!

10:17 In his office, Bob sits in front of his computer and notices a minor glitch in the marketing department's data retrieval application. There's work to be done . . . so he sends the pastry-buying suck-up to do it.

11:54 Anna has been able to work for nearly two uninterrupted hours before Davey awakens, refreshed and hungry. She jumps up, changes him, and they head into the kitchen for lunch. She places him in his high chair and asks him what he'd like to eat, even though she knows what he always wants: a baloney sandwich. "Me wan boney!" he says on cue.

11:54:30 Anna searches the refrigerator. Where's the baloney? Then she remembers that she used the last of it last night to make Chloe's lunch. Anna had meant to stop at the store on the way home from preschool, but with the traffic snafu and her conference call, it slipped her mind. Her offers of peanut butter, macaroni, or Eggos are all met with "Me wan boney!" Anna wonders why lunch has to be so difficult.

11:57 John-Michel delivers Bob's slab of ribs, which is served with spicy Asian coleslaw and garlic bread. Bob asks for extra sauce and some flavored sparkling water.

Noon To appease the heartbroken and baloney-less Davey, Anna is in the drive-thru at McDonald's where she orders him some nuggets and then adds a cheeseburger for herself. As she wolfs it down, she hopes to fit in a quick afternoon trip to the gym.

12:15 Anna stops at the dry cleaners' to pick up some of Bob's business clothes.

12:17 Bob slops barbecue sauce down the front of a newly dry-cleaned shirt.

1:00   Anna drops off Davey for a play date with Jason, the son of Trish, a good friend of hers. Finally, with some time to herself, Anna heads directly to the gym. It's crowded when she gets there and she has to wait for a StairMaster.

1:10   Bob and the other department managers meet with the company's thirty-two-year-old CEO for their weekly strategy session, which is always held during a friendly three-on-three pickup game on the company's state-of-the-art, indoor basketball court.

1:15   After only exercising for five minutes, Anna's cell phone rings. It's Clay, who informs her that he's about to shut off the power for awhile, so if she has anything on her computer . . . Crap! Anna isn't sure if she saved all her billing data. Normally, she returns to her computer after Davey eats. But today . . . She gets off the StairMaster and hurries home.

2:12   The basketball game ends; Bob and a few other managers receive congratulations from the CEO for all their hard work.

2:24   Clay is finally pulling away from the curb. Anna was able to save all her data. She checks her watch. Where did the time go? Chloe gets out of preschool in less than an hour, and Davey's play date is almost over. She's perspiring and wishes she could take another quick shower. But there's just enough time to pick up Davey and attend to another errand she has to run.

2:35   Bob has finished a steam bath and shower in the company's executive spa. He heads back to his office, scraping at the dried sauce stain on his shirt. He hopes Anna went to the cleaners today.

2:41   Anna and Davey are in Paradise Pete's Pet Emporium, where Anna selects two replacement goldfish. Davey has wandered off and begins screaming bloody murder when he somehow manages to squeeze his finger between the bars of a bird cage, and a surly cockatoo takes a nip at him.

3:10 After scurrying home, replacing the goldfish, and sticking a Band-Aid on Davey's completely unmarked finger, Anna has to hurry to pick up Chloe on time. She barely makes it, and as soon as Chloe gets in the car, Anna hands her a gym bag and tells her to get ready for softball practice. Chloe quickly and happily changes out of her school clothes and into her practice gear. Chloe is a member of the peewee softball team called the "Angels." Anna is their coach.

3:30 Practice time. There are ten 4- and 5-year-old girls on the team. But only five, Chloe included, show up on time. One of the little girls, Megan, has for some reason decided to appear at practice wearing a frilly tutu over her softball clothes. Another player, Allie, arrives and proudly shows Anna the brand-new left-handed mitt her father bought for her. Anna says that it's beautiful, even though Allie is right-handed.

Over the next fifteen minutes, the rest of the girls filter in and they have a productive and fun practice. But enjoying it more than anyone is Davey, whom all the little girls absolutely adore, and vice-versa. They keep him busy by tossing balls as far as they can; Davey runs to retrieve every one of them like a love-struck Labrador.

4:15 Bob is retrieving all data from the participants of the football pool and compiling it on one master list.

5:00 Practice is over. The parents of the girls know that they are to be picked up promptly at five.

5:20 All of the girls have been picked up except Heather, a bright but shy girl whose parents recently separated. Anna would like to get home, but her heart feels for the little girl.

5:35   Heather's mom, Lori, shows up, embarrassed and apologetic. Lori explains that her boss made her work late, even though she'd arranged to go in early on softball practice days so she could leave to pick up her daughter on time. Anna tells her not to worry, and gives Lori her cellular number, offering that if she needs to be late again, just call, and Anna will gladly take Heather home with her until Lori can pick her up.

5:40   Less than five minutes after leaving the park, the exhausted Davey is snoring in his car seat. Anna was headed for the market to pick up some things for dinner . . . and some baloney for tomorrow's lunches. But she doesn't want to wake him, and she can't leave both kids in the car while she runs into the market, so she calls Bob on his cellular.

6:21   Bob is pushing a cart down the aisle of Food King, filling a basket with items Anna requested. As he studies his list, two moms shopping nearby take notice. "Wow, what a thoughtful husband," one says to the other, "doing the grocery shopping." "Yeah," the second mom answered. "His wife is certainly lucky to have a guy like that," she adds. "I'll say," responds the first mom, noticing something about Bob with disapproval. "You'd think the least she could do would be to send him to work without a stained shirt."

6:45   Bob walks in with the groceries and kisses Anna, then the kids. Both Chloe and Davey have been bathed and are in their jammies.

6:50   Anna throws together a quick yet delicious dinner while Bob excitedly explores the three million new stations on his cable sports package.

9:00   The kids have been asleep for an hour. Bob is watching Peruvian rodeo on the bedroom TV. Anna comes in after spending ninety minutes at her computer, making up for the work time she lost today. She throws on her shorty pajamas and crawls in next to him. Bob asks her, "So, how was your day, sweetie?" And when she relates every detail, including Clay, the goldfish, and the "wrong-way" daddy, Bob can't help laughing with admiration. "How about you?" Anna asks him after she finishes.

"Aw, same ol', same ol'," he says, evasively, massaging the back of his neck.

"Hurt your neck?" she asks him.

"Nah," he covers. "Probably just a little a little work-related stress."

After they turn off the lights, Bob is glad he didn't tell Anna the real story about his neck. After hearing about her exhausting day, how could he possibly tell her that he tweaked it while screwing around in a friendly basketball game with his boss?

Bob, you are a wise man. Sleep well.

ELEVEN

SECOND-BORN CHILDREN: RULES? WHAT RULES?

Okay, so by the time your amazing first child reaches the age of about twenty-two months, you have approximately 25,000 photos showing how precious he is when he poops, pees, and pukes; when he crawls, walks, and talks. You also have hours of what you consider "classic" video footage of him smearing his face with a slice of his first birthday cake, of him being lifted onto the lap of the mall Santa, and of him throwing a petrified tantrum and being lifted *off* the lap of the mall Santa. You have pictures of his first Halloween, his first Thanksgiving, his first Christmas or Hanukkah, and probably his first Arbor, Veterans', and Groundhog Days.

Now look at all the pictures you've taken of your second child at the same age. There's one of him sitting on the front lawn, watching his dad wash the car, another one of him being pulled around like a rag doll by his darling older brother, and one of him in the family holiday card you send out to friends and family. And that's it.

In fact, our very loose and casual study suggests the ratio of photos taken of first-borns to second-borns is about 250 to 1. This is why so many "later" borns—after seeing a gazillion baby pictures of their older siblings, but virtually none of themselves—have been known to ask their moms, "Do you love Johnny more than me?" Your answer to this is, "Of course not; we love you exactly the same." (This, by the way, is not entirely accurate; see "Exactly the Same" later in this chapter.) Another question you might be asked by a less-photographed second-born is, "Mom, am I adopted?" Again, your answer should be, "Of course not." But if you choose, you can lighten the mood by adding, "Of course you're not adopted. The truth is, someone dropped you off on our front porch. You were so small and hairy, we thought you were a puppy. But when we took you inside, cleaned you up, and saw you were a person, we figured 'Aw, he's not as cute as a dog, but let's keep him anyway.'"

We think we know why we parents generally spend more time and money chronicling the early years of our first-born children so much more than those kids who follow. It's because the photos we take of our first child are not just about the child; they are also very much about us—a reminder of our lives as first-time parents.

If you are doubtful, try this experiment; the older your first child is, the more effective the experiment will be. For example, let's say he's now eighteen. Take out one of the forty albums you have of his first year on earth and pick a photo of any important event, such as his first birthday party. The picture depicts you and your husband sitting with your baby at your kitchen table in the apartment you rented back then. Also at the party are a neighbor couple and their seventeen-month-old daughter.

As you look at the photo after all these years, don't be surprised if you spend very little time, or any at all, talking about your child. Even though the big event was all about his first birthday, you will have little or no recollection of where you bought that cute outfit he's wearing, what present you gave him, or even where you bought his cake.

Instead, the conversation will go like this:

"Oh, God," you say to your husband, "remember that horrible kitchen wallpaper?"

"Yeah," he answers. "Look how crooked it is. What were we thinking when we put that up?"

"'More beers'?" you laugh.

"Nice hair, hon." he comments, pointing at your $10 coif. "All you need is a pair of ice skates and I'd swear it was Dorothy Hamel."

You study him in the picture. Minus twenty-five pounds, he was actually a bit skinny back then. He's wearing a tight black T-shirt, form-fitting jeans, and moussed hair with a rakish curl creeping down his forehead.

"Well, look who's talking, Mr. Bon Jovi," you laugh.

Then you talk about the neighbors, Howard and LeAnn (or was it Harold and Laney?). This leads you to recall your landlord and her husband, the Duffys, who you called the Puffys, because they each went through at least two packs of Marlboros a day. Then you move on to the mom and pop deli down the street, and finally, to the time your Mercury Comet caught fire in the carport.

But nothing about your son and his birthday.

And as you move on to other photos of your child, it will go the same way—very little about him, but a lot about you. And that's okay. That's also a big reason why you don't have loads of photos of your children who follow your first-born. You've already celebrated a child's first birthday. And your second child's "Baby's First Christmas" is not "Your First Baby's First Christmas." Although it may be a case of "been there, done that," don't feel guilty. It's only human.

If you still have any doubt about the existence of this phenomenon, here's one more thing to consider:

Remember when your cute first-born was about fifteen months old and began walking? And remember the time that she was playing in the living room and tossed a ball under the heavy oak dining table? And remember how she crawled under the table and retrieved the ball and then stood up and whacked her head against one of the metal braces under the table?

Waaaaah! Then she tumbled to the ground in heap, as though she'd been leveled by a cannonball. Waaaaaaah! Waaaahhh! Set loose the banshees! You run to her and pull her out from under the table and feel her head. Ohmigod! There's already a bump starting to form! And what's that trace of liquid you feel? You check your finger, and you see a speck of blood! Somebody help! Your daughter could be bleeding to death.

You frantically call your pediatrician, even though it's nearly 8 P.M. Of course you get his office recording, so you leave a rambling message. He calls you back fifteen minutes later from a restaurant where he's having dinner with friends. You wonder what kind of doctor would dare have dinner with friends while your daughter could be in very critical condition. Sure, her crying is tapering off and there's no more blood, but this could still be very serious. The pediatrician says it's probably a harmless bump; babies' skulls are made to withstand such things. You can't believe this guy's cavalier attitude; you make a note to check out exactly where he went to medical school.

An hour later, you and your husband are in the emergency room. Your daughter is sleeping, and this worries you because you read somewhere that people can lose consciousness when they have a concussion.

You go to the intake nurse and ask yet again how long it will be. She repeats that there are people ahead of you, and then has the nerve to call in a man who fell from his roof to his cement driveway while putting up Christmas lights. Where the heck are her priorities?

At 11 P.M., a highly trained E.R. physician is finally examining your daughter. He checks out her eye motion, her reflexes, and tries to locate what you call the "huge gash" atop her head. Everything checks out perfectly normal; she's fine. Your daughter has apparently forgotten the entire incident and is now only interested in playing with his stethoscope. You get home after midnight and gently place your brave and tough little girl in her crib.

Whew, that was a close call.

Now, it's two years later. Second-born child, but the same dining table.

Whack! Waaaaahhh!

You drag her from under the table and feel the bump forming. There's a little more blood than last time.

"Honey, could you get some ice," you call to your husband calmly. Then you take your wailing child and hold her tight. "Come on, sweetie. Time for *American Idol*.

Crisis solved.

EXACTLY THE SAME? NOT EXACTLY

As we mentioned earlier, it's not entirely accurate when we say that we love our children "exactly the same." We may love them "equally" but it's very nearly impossible to love them exactly the same.

For example, let's say you're the mother of two: a twenty-three-year-old son and a twenty-year-old daughter. Your precious first-born son was a joy to raise. He was a model son: polite, attentive, and extremely intelligent, graduating from high school with honors and receiving a full scholarship to a prestigious university in the east to study molecular biology, with an ultimate goal of helping to find cures to some of the world's most devastating diseases. He gradated in three years, after which he earned his PhD.

Recently, he was able to parlay his extensive and expensive education into a career as a professional dog walker—a calling he tells you "is much more in line with his life flow." He lives on a ramshackle tobacco farm in Connecticut with a girl named Rhonda, who has two kids and is twelve years older than he. He recently cut his hair so that it spells out the word "Mojo" and has taken to sleeping in a teepee, awaiting the arrival of "The Others." But he's always been a wonderful son, and you love him.

Your twenty-year-old daughter, on the other hand, spent all of her teen years trying to make you crazy. She experimented with drugs, hung out with a questionable crowd, and did everything she could to make Madonna seem like Mother Teresa. Then, at seventeen, she was diagnosed with a reading disability. You were able to convince her to seek educational therapy, and although she fought it at first, the wonder of books and literature eventually opened up a brand new world for her. She didn't graduate high school with her class, but she studied tirelessly to earn her GED only four months behind schedule. She enrolled at a community college and was recently accepted into the Education Department at the University of Michigan. You are so proud of her.

So you see, we don't always love each of our children exactly the same. But we love them equally, even though it's not always easy.

And now, a final thought on the first-born/second-born dynamic. Here's a list of rules that a new mom might have for her first-born:

- *Sit up straight.*
- *Don't play with your food.*
- *Keep your hands away from the stove.*
- *Don't pick your nose.*
- *Eat your vegetables.*
- *Don't bite your fingernails.*
- *Always remember to say "please" and "thank you."*
- *Don't strangle the cat.*
- *Keep your elbows off the table.*
- *Don't chew with your mouth full.*

And now, for a second-born:
Go to sleep.

So if you're a mom with one child, and are contemplating enriching your life with a second, here are two very useful Mom Rules for you:

1. Get your camera ready and be sure to take plenty of pictures of your second child, no matter how redundant it might feel. It will save you a lot of questions later on.
2. Don't forget to tape some protective padding under that dining room table.

TWELVE

MOM CARPOOL GUIDELINES: THE ZEN OF SCHLEPPING

Every mom with school-age kids and a gas-guzzling SUV is acutely aware of the advantages of belonging to a reliable carpool. A group of two or three moms sharing the transportation load can free up oodles of time for you, allowing you to attend to other important mom stuff . . . like painting the guest bathroom that your husband started but never finished, trying to crack your thirteen-year-old daughter's password to make sure she isn't receiving any inappropriate email, and taking your mother-in-law to the podiatrist to have her neglected, talonlike toenails clipped yet again.

But as liberating and as time-saving as a carpool can be, you should remember that getting involved in one is much like joining any other business or social group; it's always best to know the players before you jump into the game. And while forming a carpool with like-minded mom friends is usually a good thing, there is one pitfall to be aware of: All it takes is one instance of another carpool mom unnecessarily scolding or disciplining your child for something she says she didn't do, and it's entirely possible that you could be removing one name from your Facebook "friends" list.

Just a word to the wise.

So how do you know that you're getting into a carpool that can be productive and relatively hassle-free? Simple: You should do some casual screening of the other moms to determine if they'd make reliable carpool partners. For example, any mom who sports a bumper sticker reading "My Child Was Student of the Month at Oakdale Elementary School" is a probably a keeper, because this is an excellent indication that she places a high value on academic achievement and makes certain to get her child to school on time every day, rain or shine. But there's a baby fly in the ointment here. Just to be on the safe side, make sure this mom doesn't take her child to school *too early* every day (say 7 A.M. for an 8:15 bell), so that the little genius can spend extra time in the reference library or with the Advanced Trigonometry Club. You know that getting your kid to school at 7 A.M. is about as likely as getting your husband to a scrapping party.

Also, if you have any doubts at all about this bumper-sticker mom, you should check school records to see exactly what month it was that her child was honored. Here's why: Common sense dictates that it's more of an achievement to be selected "Student of the Month" during a month that has a full thirty-one days—like October, December, or January—because a child has to be better, longer. And while being selected the top student of a thirty-day month is no small accomplishment, you might want to reconsider this mother's carpool participation if her child was honored in February.

Another good candidate for any carpool is what we call a S.I.M.—a Super-Involved Mom. This is a mother who spends more time at her child's school than the principal and the custodian combined. She's on the board of the PTA; she's a "room mother," a playground supervisor, runs the fund-raising candy bar sale, and also directs and cho-reographs the annual school play, for which she also sews many of the costumes. You know the type . . . she's kind of a pain, but since she's always at the school, she is not the least bit inconvenienced if you have a carpool emergency (like if your stylist changes your highlighting appointment from 10:30 A.M. to 3 P.M.).

"No problem," she'll say when you call with some com-plicated story involving your plumbing and a sick pet. "I'll just keep the kids at school with me until you can get here. They can help me steam-clean the carpets in the pre-k room, then we'll get started painting new lines in the fac-ulty parking lot."

When you arrive at school later that day, your child is upset and exhausted. You'll feel a little guilty because you selfishly abrogated your responsibility. But you get over it when your husband gets home, eyes you, and wraps his arms around your waist. "Hey, Mama," he says amorously. "You do somethin' to your hair?"

On the other side of the coin, there are few warning signs that a mom may not be a good fit for your carpool:

- Any mom who drives a Yugo, a Fiat, or similarly unreliable vehicle made in any country whose men enjoy wearing dark socks with brief swimming trunks (unless you want your child stranded alongside a busy freeway while she tries to retrieve her transmission from the fast lane).
- Any mom who sporadically shows up wearing a neck brace for whiplash.
- Any mom who you suspect might have a less than ster-ling driving record. An innocent way to find out would be to say to her casually, "It's not fair. Just because I

tapped someone in the supermarket parking lot, my insurance company raised my rates to over $200 a month!" If her response is, "$200 a month?! Shoot, I pay that a day," it's time to move on.

Once you've assembled a few reliable moms for carpool duty, your next step is to get to know the personalities of their children. You may already be familiar with one or two of them, because you're friendly with their parents. You've talked to these children at birthday parties, family barbecues, or youth sports functions. But no matter how well you know these youngsters, there's nothing like a season of cold, early-morning car rides to give you the opportunity to really and truly bond.

First, you need to remember that the largest chunk of the standard school year takes place during these and in most places in the United States, these are the coldest, dampest, darkest times of the year. If they weren't, fall and winter would be called summer or late spring. Or Bermuda.

Added to the mix is the fact that most schools open for business between 7:30 and 8:00 A.M., five days a week. Ergo, it only requires some basic math to see that everyone involved in the carpool—schleppers and students alike—are likely to be understandably surly, because they are obligated to begin 75 percent of their early mornings doing something they don't want to be doing. Most school mornings, a child would much rather stay in bed than be crammed into a cold, metal sneeze-tube with other kids who have nothing more exciting to look forward to in their day than a squashed peanut butter sandwich and recess . . . especially a recess that requires mittens, mufflers, scarves, and snow boots.

Moms, on the other hand, would much rather be sitting next to the hearth, enjoying a hot beverage with Matt Lauer. But that's not an option; you are a carpooling mom and you must fulfill your sacred responsibilities. If you shirk, the children will suffer; the natural balance of things will be set spinning; and most importantly, that do-everything S.I.M. mom will start a rumor about you and late-night carousing.

So embrace the beast. The next time it's your morning to drive, leap out of bed with a smile, even though it's drizzling and you suddenly remember that you forgot to close the car windows last night. Throw on your most comfortable sweat suit over your flannel pajamas, and then jam a ball cap over your flailing, morning hair. (Note: Putting on a bra for such an occasion is optional. If it's really, really cold in your bedroom in the morning, do you really want to put yourself through that?) Besides, with all the layers you'll be wearing by the time you leave the house, you could cover your breasts with two construction cones and no one would notice. But on the other hand, if you choose not to slip on a bra, it's possible that you could hear your mother's haunting admonition from years earlier: "Okay, fine, Ms. Bra-less, but if you get in an accident . . . "

So you hurry outside and start the car, setting the heater control to "Death Valley, August," and scamper back inside to get your child ready. By the time you're ready to leave, the car is warm and toasty, although the circulation system is sending dog hair flying everywhere.

And once you've picked up the kids and are headed for school, try something different. Instead of riding in numb silence, try talking to the kids, or even singing silly songs. Of course, *your* thirteen-year-old daughter will be absolutely mortified by this, but certainly not as much as she was the morning your husband filled in for you. He was listening to a classic rock station and belted out Foreigner's "I Want to Know What Love Is" all the way to the head of the drop-off lane . . . with the windows down.

Engaging the children during your carpool travels is good for everyone. As you get to know them better, they will become much more comfortable talking with you, a real, live adult. And as this relationship grows, the children will let their guards down more and more and will discuss all sorts of things in front of you. This is a huge asset for you, because you now have the opportunity to gather troves of valuable intelligence information: who the "easy" girls are, what certain history teacher is secretly courting the head of the music department, what Mrs. Caruso told her sex education class.

And maybe, since your daughter's BFF is also in your carpool, you could eventually trick her into parting with the ultimate piece of intelligence: your daughter's email password.

THIRTEEN

YOUR MOM HAS TOLD YOU A THOUSAND TIMES . . . AND SHE'S NOT DONE YET

See, there's this thing about belonging to the Mom Club—it's a lifetime affiliation; there is no revoking your membership. There is no way we can resign from the responsibilities of being a mom, even though the behavior of our children sometimes make us wish we could.

We wear many hats in life, and we can change or toss away virtually any of them whenever we choose . . . or when the fit just isn't right anymore. We can stop being a wife. We can stop being a schoolteacher or an accountant, a minister or a pole dancer. We can stop being a redhead or a Dead Head; a liberal or a conservative; a carnivore or a vegetarian; a rocker or a stalker. But stop being a mom? Can you imagine?

"Hi, Joan, long time no see. How are the kids?"

"Kids? Oh, no; I retired from that about six years ago. I'm raising llamas now."

Should you foolishly believe that there is an expiration date on the milk carton of mom-hood, I overheard the following conversation between two women not long ago:

"Mary, would you and Joe like to catch a movie Friday night?"

"Friday?" Oh, shoot, we can't; we're going to our son's baseball game."

"Little League?" the first woman asked with surprise.

"No. An 'Over 40' league. His team's playing for the championship, and Billy's pitching."

And how about our neighbor, Dana, who recently took her daughter and some friends to Disneyland to celebrate the amusement park's fiftieth anniversary. So what's the big deal about that? Well, Dana's daughter is also fifty, born on the same date Disneyland first opened its gates.

So you see, it often helps to remember that "mother" is just "smother'" minus an "s." This goes a long way toward explaining why moms of one generation feel compelled to offer parenting advice to moms of the next. If you're a relatively new mom, your mother's unsolicited input will surely rankle you at times, but we suggest you roll with it. Because as you start racking up more mom miles yourself, your mother's suggestions and comments will bother you less and less. In fact, believe it or not, some of them may eventually begin to make sense. Or not.

But either way, expecting your mom to stop with the advice is like expecting your husband of ten-plus years to touch you in just the right spot every single time. And if you really expect that to happen, you may need a far more serious book than this.

And if you think your mom's observations and critiques about your parenting won't begin until *after* your baby is born, think again. For example, when she finds out how much you paid for your baby stroller, she won't be able to contain herself.

"Eight hundred dollars for a stroller?! When you were a baby, your father and I only paid $750 for a used Ford station wagon! What's this stroller got, its own chauffeur?"

And wait till you tell her that you're planning to have a natural childbirth in a birth center where your doctor will be working with Nina and Joan, your two doulas.

"Your two what?" your mom asks, miming that she misheard by digging imaginary wax from her ear. You explain that a doula is a birthing assistant who is trained to help you prenatally and also during delivery with positioning, breathing, and massaging.

"Massaging? You're having a baby, not going to a spa!" Then she adds, "And take the epidural! What are you, nuts?"

You can also expect her opinions on the use of pacifiers, the name you've chosen for the baby, and how—when *she* was pregnant—she managed to gain far less weight than you have.

Once your baby is born, it is only natural that you will begin using parenting phrases and techniques that weren't around when your mother was mothering you. But you should be prepared for sarcastic comments or at least deep-throated moans from your mom when you spout them to her.

Say your mother drops by one afternoon to ask you if she could take your five-year-old daughter, Jenny, for a quick trip to the nearby mall:

YOU: "Sorry, Mom, but Jenny's not home. She's at a play date."

YOUR MOM: "A what?"

YOU: "A play date."

YOUR MOM: "What the devil is that?"

YOU: "She made a date to go play with Lisa."

YOUR MOM: "Lisa? Doesn't she live right next door?"

YOU: "Yep, we set it up last week."

YOUR MOM: "Last week? Are you kiddin'? Why couldn't Jenny just run next door, knock on Lisa's door, and say, 'Hey, want to play?' That was good enough for you and your friend Sara."

YOU: "That's not the way we do things these days, Mom." (You try not to sound too superior.)

YOUR MOM: "Why not?"

YOU: "Because what if Lisa were busy? Jenny could take that as a sign of rejection."

Your mother stares at you, numb. She wants to say more, but she decides to let it go. Almost.

YOUR MOM: "Okay," she says, turning to go. "I need to get to the mall and back before dinner, so when Jenny gets home, could you have her phone me? Or should I set up a call date?"

And then she leaves.

Later, Jenny hasn't yet called your mom. Your phone rings.

YOU: "Oh, hey, Mom. No, Jenny can't talk to you right now. She's having a time-out."

YOUR MOM: "A time-out from what? Are she and her friend still playing?"

YOU: "No, Mom. A time-out is punishment."

YOUR MOM: "Like in hockey? What did she do? Knock her friend's tooth loose with a stick?"

YOU: "When Jenny came back from her play date she was all hyper and started misbehaving. So I gave her a time-out."

YOUR MOM: "Oh, so you sent her to her bedroom."

YOU: "Her bedroom? Mom, everything she enjoys is in there." (Once again you hear an air or superiority creeping into your voice.) "She's in the laundry room."

YOUR MOM: "Laundry room? You're making a five-year-old do the wash?"

YOU: "No, Mom. She's sitting on the dryer."

YOUR MOM: "Doing what?"

YOU: "Thinking about the consequences of her actions."

At this point, there is silence on your mother's end of the line. Finally she speaks.

YOUR MOM: "Sweetie, have you been drinking?"

YOU: "Of course not," you answer, insulted.

YOUR MOM: "Well, maybe you should. It might loosen you up."

And then she says she'll talk to you tomorrow and hangs up.

So should there ever come a time when your mom's willingness to offer parenting advice is about to make your head explode, just remember that it's an age-old tradition, deep-rooted in every mother's DNA.

Exactly like it is in yours.

You just don't know it yet.

FOURTEEN

BRAGGING RIGHTS ... AND WRONGS

From the beginning of time, moms have been lauding their children's talents and accomplishments, no matter how obscure, inconsequential, or dubious they might seem to other moms. Eve, best known for Cain and Abel, also had another son named Seth, about whom she once boasted, "He may not get as much publicity as his brothers, but Seth is an absolutely wonderful listener."

And eons later, Atilla the Hun's mother—Janet the Hun—told her friends at a cosmetics party, "My son is so thoughtful. I told him I needed a new set of teeth and he sent me some in two days. All I had to do was remove them from the skull."

And in the early 1930s, Emma Parker, mom of infamous bandit and killer Bonnie Parker (Bonnie and Clyde), bragged while defending her daughter's life of crime to a cashier at her local 7-Eleven: "Yeah? Well, let's see if your daughter could get on *anybody's* 'Most Wanted' list!"

These days, moms can begin singing their child's praises even before they come into the world.

"Isn't she adorable?" you say to a coworker as you hold up a copy of your very first sonogram for her to view. She stares at it blankly, trying to be polite as she's forced to stare

at an image that looks like a Rorschach test after too many margaritas.

Then, several months later, you want to share the amazing feeling you feel when your eight-month-old fetus frolics inside you.

"Have you ever felt such amazing leg power?" you gush to the woman whose hand you've placed on your belly. "I'm thinking she may grow up to be a famous dancer. Or a soccer player." The woman forces a smile, then quickly removes her hand and says, "Well, good luck with the baby. Nice meeting you."

Although bragging about one's children will never end, there are some right and wrong ways to go about it.

Mom Rule: When you are with women friends who don't yet have children of their own, do not try to inject all of your child's amazing accomplishments into every conversation. (This will be extremely difficult to do, but do it you must . . . unless you want these friends to soon become your ex-friends.)

Let me tell you a story about three longtime girlfriends whom I'll call Sue, Deb, and Melissa. Sue has been married for three years, but she and her husband have decided to hold off having kids until they're more financially flexible. Deb is engaged (finally!) and her wedding is only a month away. Melissa is married and is the only mom. She has a nine-month-old son, just like you. And coincidentally, Melissa is thirty-three, just like you. She also drives a blue SUV—again just like you.

But of course, Melissa is not you. No way.

The three young women are out, having a nice lunch together, and Deb is going over a list of things she still has to do for her wedding, including selecting centerpieces for the tables at the reception.

"I can't decide whether to go with fresh cut or potted flowers."

"Fa-wahs," Melissa-the-mom says with a proud laugh.

"Pardon?" asks Sue.

"Fah-wahs. That's how Jackson says 'flowers,'" Melissa explains. "Can you believe it? Only nine months old, and he's already saying words like that. He's extremely gifted verbally."

Melissa doesn't notice as Deb and Sue exchange bemused looks.

"I think live flowers are nice," Sue says to Deb, getting the conversation back on track. "They're eco-friendly, and people can take 'em home, plant 'em, and always think of your wedding day."

"Good point," Deb agrees. She makes a note of this and moves on to the next item on her list. "One month to go, and Dan and I still haven't decided on wedding rings."

"That reminds me," Melissa says quickly. "If you're looking for a ring bearer, Jackson would be really cute."

Deb is taken aback by this offer. "He sure would," she says politely. "But I really think a ring bearer should be able to walk, don't you?"

"Sure, but the wedding's not till next month," Melissa says cheerily. "Last night, Jax crawled over to the coffee table, grabbed it, and pulled himself to his feet. The kid is so strong. Who knows what he'll be doing in four weeks? He'll probably be able to sprint down the aisle."

"That's a nice thought," Deb says, "but I already asked my nephew."

"Oh, right," Melissa answers, trying to hide her hurt feelings. "But I've been to a few weddings where they've had two ring bearers, you know."

Later, when the women are outside waiting for the valet to bring Melissa's car—she drove the three of them—her phone rings. It's her husband, calling with amazing news.

"What?" she screeches into the phone, excited. "Jackson? Really? Oh, how precious!" she yells loud enough for everyone on the block to hear. "Okay, we'll be right there!" She hangs up and gives Deb and Sue the 4-1-1. She explains that after Jackson woke up from his nap, he and Melissa's husband went to their local pet store to buy dog food. "And while they were there," she tells Deb and Sue, bursting her buttons, "Jackson was approached by a photographer who's shooting the store's upcoming 'Kids and Canines' calendar. He wants to pose Jax with an Irish Setter and shoot him right away!"

Then she impatiently yells at a nearby valet, "Where the hell's my car?"

Deb and Sue exchange worried glances; is this going where they're afraid it might be going? After all, they did hear Melissa say to her husband, "*We'll* be right there," not "*I'll* be right there."

When Melissa's car arrives seconds later, she says to her friends, "Let's go; we don't want to miss this."

Before Deb and Sue can squirm out of it and call for a cab, Melissa has herded them into her car and away they go.

At 6:30 that evening, Deb and Sue have had it. They've been on their feet in the pet store for over four hours and worse, they've had to stand near the grooming section, and they both reek of flea dip. Melissa, meanwhile, has made three trips home, each time to get a different, cuter outfit for Jackson.

The photographer finally gets his picture at 7:30, and a weary but ecstatic Melissa drives her two tight-lipped friends home.

During the month leading up to Deb's wedding, Melissa puts in several calls to her friends, but Deb is always too busy with preparations to talk for very long. It's the same when Melissa calls Sue, who always seems to be "on the other line."

They all get along well at the wedding, at least until late in the evening when Melissa takes the dance floor with Jackson, holding him in her arms and whirling him about like a miniature Fred Astaire. In her enthusiasm to show everyone what a fine and precious little dancer he is, she begins spinning him, sending his legs flying in all directions. Unfortunately, one of those directions was where the Best Man was about to take a sip of champagne, when the rock-hard heel of one Jackson's brand new "big boy shoes" clipped his glass, which banged against his front tooth, chipping it horribly.

In the months following Deb's wedding, Melissa heard from her two friends less and less, and assumed that it was because she had a child and neither of them did. And she may have been exactly right. But just in case, here's a bit of advice: Try not to be a Melissa . . . not that you ever would.

In an ironic footnote, Melissa and Sue ran into each other in an OB-GYN office a couple of years later; Melissa was pregnant with Jackson's little sister, while Sue and her husband had decided to jump into the parenthood waters for the first time. They saw each other frequently, and Sue often sought out Melissa's advice on birth classes, pediatricians, and the best brands of baby equipment.

They delivered within two weeks of each other, and occasionally the families would get together socially. But that began to phase out when Sue's baby reached the age of nine months or so.

"Jeez, what a pain Sue is," Melissa said. "She thinks her kid is so darned precious."

Spoken like the veteran mother of a second born.

★　★　★　★　★

Here are a few other bragging taboos you should be aware of as you schuss your way through the moguls of motherhood:

You're at your eight-year-old daughter Sara's softball game. Although she's clearly the best player on the team (even her coach finally agrees with you), Sara is happily sitting on the bench for an inning so that all of her teammates get a chance to play. An opposing player hits a popup to the shortstop, Sara's regular position, but her replacement botches it, taking it off the forehead. After some tears and some TLC from her coaches, all the parents in the bleachers applaud her effort, with you leading the cheers.

"Nice try, Beth," you yell to her. That's nice.

But before you can stop yourself, you holler even louder:

"Maybe Sara can work with you so don't screw up next time."

Not so nice.

Next, you're in your child's fifth grade classroom for "Back to School Night." You're sitting at your son's desk, perusing some tests he's taken thus far in the year. A woman sitting next to you is doing the same with her child's papers, and she's so obviously proud of her daughter's academic acuity that she feels all the other parents should know about it as well. "Ninety-five in Math . . . wow!" she blurts for all to hear. "Ninety-four in Social Studies . . . amazing!" she adds.

After a few more of these exclamations, you can take no more. "Your daughter must be quite a student," you say innocently.

"Oh, yes," she says without a thought. Then she holds up her daughter's tests. "Every one of her tests is in the nineties," she declares with the volume, intensity, and passion of Lincoln delivering the Gettysburg Address.

"That's wonderful," you say sweetly. But there's not one granule of sugar in what comes out of your mouth next. "I guess for some parents, '90s' is the new '100.'"

Then you drop your child's folder of perfect test scores on her desk and move on.

Victory is sweet! Bragging . . . not so much.

None of this is to suggest that every time you tell a story about your child you are bragging. Of course not. In fact, "bragging" is defined as "boasting; indulging in self-glorification," and with children, usually involves athletics, grades, or other special talents. In other words, *bragging* nearly always focuses on a child's *performance*.

But moms sharing stories about what their children think—or say—doesn't seem like bragging; it's normally for the pure amusement of it.

When we conducted our interviews for *Mom Rules*, we asked hundreds of moms to answer two questions . . . and two questions only. Not three. Not four. Two. These were:

1. Do you have any amusing Mom Rules that you've come up with?
2. How would you or your child complete the following sentence: "My mom rules because . . . "

We received thousands of delightful and insightful responses. But we soon saw that most moms didn't stop at these two questions. We began receiving scores of unsolicited anecdotes from moms about the funny, quirky things that came out of their childrens' mouths.

In reading these stories, we noticed something very, very surprising: Moms weren't telling us the funny things their *kids* said; they were telling the funny thing their *sons* said. That's right. Virtually every mom's anecdote was about Johnny, or Jimmy, or Adam . . . There was not a mention of a Judy, a Missy, or a Jane. This led us to what we think is the most important sociological discovery since Masters and Johnson and all their "erogenous zone" stuff. We call it:

THE FUNNY-BOY PHENOMENON

For some reason, moms think that their boys are intrinsically funny. We're not sure why this is but suspect that this perception is based on one important factor: Most moms did not grow up as boys themselves. And now that moms have these entertaining little bundles of XY chromosomes available to them 24/7, it opens up a whole new world for them. A world of impulsiveness, a world lacking clarity of thought, a world full of whoopee cushions.

Perhaps the motherly perception—and acceptance—of sons as Funny Boys accounts for the disproportionate number of male comedians to their female counterparts. Or why there is a Bozo the Clown, but no Babette. We're also quite certain that this explains why the Village Idiot is never wearing a dress.

So now, with a tip of our caps to Art Linkletter, here are just a few stories sent to us by moms who are certain that "Sons Say the Darndest Things."

The following are from five-year-old Brady Goar and

may offer some insight into the thought process of a male his age . . . if, indeed, there is such a thing:

- *"Mom, can I have eggs for breakfast? Not the real kind, the kind that sorta look like popcorn."*
- *When Brady and his dad returned from soccer practice, his mom asked how it went. "I scored four girls . . . I mean four goals. I was just kidding about the girls, Mom."*
- *When Brady's mom asked him if she could borrow his pen, Brady answered, "Not right now, Mom, I need it to tap my head while I'm thinking."*

Lest you assume that this type of circuitous, logic-bending thinking will improve as your male child gets older, you should consider this example of XY thinking from Mike, an eight-year-old we know well:

Mike returned home from a friend's birthday party, caked in dirt and sweat, telling his mom what a great party it was. His friend's mother took all eight boys to a hilly park, where they chose sides and played "Army." They spent the whole summer day doing what eight-year-old boys enjoy most: tumbling down dusty hills after they'd been "shot" by the enemy.

Mike's mom opined that he could use a bath; Mike immediately agreed, and soon she heard the bathtub filling. Twenty minutes later, she heard the tub draining; then, curiously, she heard Mike turn on the shower.

When he finally emerged from the bathroom, she asked him if, in fact, he'd taken both a bath and a shower.

"Yep," he said. "The bath was to get the dirt off. The shower was for the smell."

If you need further evidence that some things don't change with age, here are two ruminations from our neighbor, twelve-year-old Christopher:

- *When Christopher was studying about the weather phenomenon, El Nino, his mother told him he'd been born smack dab in the middle of it. "It had rained for weeks, except for the day we brought you home from the hospital." Then she added. "But that day, it was sunny and warm." "'Course, Mom; that's 'cause the gods were happy."*

- *Christopher and his mom were talking about a boy in his fifth grade class who had a girlfriend. "Do you have a girlfriend?" his mother asked him. "I don't want a girlfriend," Christopher replied. "I want to be rich!"*

And here's a story from our good friend Ann Sayre, an energetic, always-on-the-go mother of three teenage boys. This one involves her fifteen-year-old, Wyatt:

After a hot day at school that included a full, sweaty hour of P.E., Wyatt had the opportunity to help out on a movie set, a field he hopes to pursue. He didn't have time to come home and shower after school, and when he finally got home that night, he was too bushed to do anything but go right to bed. "I'll shower in the morning," he promised his mom.

The next day, Ann's "to-do" list was chock full, and she left the house at 7:30 a.m. It was a school off-day for Wyatt, so she let him sleep in. But she left him a note: "Be sure to shower!" she wrote, adding that she'd be home to pick him up at 2 p.m. to have him back at the movie set at three.

Of course, like any 2010 mom, Ann always runs a little late; she pulled into her driveway at 2:20, honked her horn, and Wyatt sprinted out. But as he approached the car, Ann saw that his hair was an oily mess. If this kid took a shower, *she thought,* he did it in a full wetsuit.

"What happened to your shower?" she asked him. Wyatt uncomfortably told her that when he woke up at noon, the family's

housekeeper was there, and Wyatt was too embarrassed to get in the shower. So he just changed his clothes.

"Jeez, you're gonna stink!" she told him.

"No, I'm not, Mom," Wyatt answered confidently. "I sprayed myself with Febreze!"

Still any doubts about sons being just a little bit off-center? If so, try to imagine your fifteen-year-old daughter doing such a thing. Would never happen, right? Of course not; she would have absolutely no idea what Febreze is. Or where one keeps it.

And finally, children—particularly young male ones—are infamous for blurting out things at the wrong times . . . and these things are usually completely unrelated to what's going on around them.

We heard this story a number of years ago, and it still makes us laugh (Note: It contains a word that some might find objectionable. We've camouflaged it as best we can.):

Like most two-year-olds, Brendan was still learning the finer points of English pronunciation the day his mom took him to the doctor for a routine checkup and inoculation. When the doctor administered the shot, Brendan didn't flinch, whine, or shed a tear. Instead, he felt this offered him the perfect opportunity to tell his mom something extremely important.

"Maw-Maw, Dada ded wuh kit," he blurted.

While this was nothing but gobbledygook to the doctor, a mom has the ability to understand every word that comes from her child's mouth. So she interpreted for the doctor's benefit. "That's right, honey," she said to the two-year-old. "Dada is working."

Bur Brendan was insistent. "No, Maw-Maw . . . Dada ded wuh kit!" he repeated, louder this time.

"I know," his mom answered again, smiling uncomfortably. "Dada is working."

Brendan was now thoroughly frustrated with his mom's inability to understand what he was saying. That had never happened before.

"NO, MAW-MAW!" Brendan yelled, pronouncing each syllable clearly. "DADA DED WUH KIT!"

Fortunately for Brendan's mom, the doctor had a busy schedule; so he gave Brendan a lollipop, then left to tend to another patient. But Brendan was intent on getting his message across to his mother . . .

"Maw-Maw, Dada ded . . . "

But Brendan's mom quickly covered his mouth. "Yes, Brendan, I know," she whispered. "Dada said 'f★★★ it.' It's a bad word and he is very sorry, and I guarantee he will never say it again."

Why Brendon saw a doctor's appointment as the ideal time to mention his father's misbehavior is anyone's guess.

But hearing what comes out of the mouths of little boys may help you better understand the thought process of the little boy you call your husband. And understanding is the first step to solving the mystery of why he says certain things when he does—like last Friday night when the two of you went to see a documentary on climate change. It was at the most riveting and heartbreaking moment of the film, where a mother polar bear dies, leaving behind three unattended babies, that your husband whispered in your ear, "Do we have any pancake batter at home?"

But then again, some things may never be understood.

FIFTEEN

HERE TODAY, GONE TOMORROW

Moms have said that the most life-changing decision they ever made was to have children. And many of these moms agree that their second most important decision was to continue to claim these children as their own, even when they came home with tattoos, body piercings, and boyfriends named "Snake Puppy."

But through all the good times and bad, responsible parents stayed focused on their mission: to love and nurture their kids with the hope that they would eventually mature into responsible, compassionate, and contributing adults. If and when that happens, we can congratulate ourselves for having provided them with a solid education that will allow them to strive and succeed (and to use Craigslist to find a nice apartment to rent—one not too close to home, and preferably one with its own washer and dryer). And while moms know that it's the nature of things for their baby birds to eventually leave the nest, it can be a shock to the system when it actually happens . . . particularly if the departing bird is your *only* bird. Or your last one.

The emotional impact of a child moving out normally depends on whether the move is permanent or temporary. The most common variety of a permanent move is . . . GOTCHA!!! You see, when it comes to our kids, there is no such thing as a permanent move. Because with today's slumping economy and bulging divorce rate, even children who have been long gone are finding themselves limping back to the nest. They know that in times of emergency, your door is always open—regardless of how many times you've tried to fool them by changing your locks, your security code, your address, or your identity.

Because you know that a mom never retires from being a mom, you find a way to accommodate your loveable lost soul. But be careful, because this can be a very slippery slope. Our friends' thirty-seven-year-old son moved back home after a bitter and financially devastating divorce, followed by a job loss. He swore the move was temporary and would only last until he could get back on his feet again. That was four years ago, and he's still there; the only time he gets on his feet is to greet the pizza delivery guy.

The most common temporary move occurs when a child goes off to college; he will be gone most of the time, but will still visit home just enough to stop you from finally putting new odor-free carpet in his bedroom. The frequency of these visits is determined by which one of two categories of college students your child falls into: "Surprisers" or "Curbies." Surprisers attend college at least ninety miles from home, but no farther away than four hundred miles. Because they can get home by car, they often show up unannounced and yell, "Surprise!" These students are easily identified by their full laundry bags and empty gas tanks.

"Curbies," on the other hand, attend a college that is more than four hundred miles away, which means they generally need to take a plane, train, or bus to get home. This, of course, requires that you pick them up at some sort of terminal or station, often at the busiest travel times, so they've learned to wait for you at the curb.

A Curbie normally returns home only two or three times a school year, which some moms see as a huge downside. But once these moms reacquaint themselves with their life before children—a life of sleeping in on weekends, going to late afternoon movies without having to hurry home and fix Sloppy Joes, and being the only one to wear her own clothes—they soon come to see this as a huge upside as well.

But this doesn't mean that saying good-bye to a Surpriser is easy. Even though they will likely be popping in whenever they miss you, your cooking, or your gold cards, the initial realization that they're really gone can be very traumatic on a mom. Let's say you're the mom of a typical Surpriser. Let's say her name is Amanda. She just turned eighteen, and she'll be leaving for college for the very first time.

Amanda received her acceptance in mid-May to her first choice of colleges and is scheduled to move into her on-campus dorm at 12:30 P.M., September 1. In early July, you and she drove the 176 miles to the school to take a prearranged tour. Walking about the storied campus, you notice the ivied walls, the venerable statues, and the feeling of community. Your daughter notices the fitness center and the food courts.

You visit her unfurnished dorm room and immediately take out your tape measure. After confirming with your guide that the room's color will not change before September 1, Amanda snaps about three thousand pictures with her cell phone.

The next two months are a wonderful time for both of you as you team up to make sure she has everything she needs to make her new nest every bit as comfortable as her old one. As you shop for curtains, bed linens, and a new laptop, September 1 seems so far away.

Then, on August 31, at 11:15 P.M., you spring up in bed. It's not like you were asleep, because how can any responsible, caring mom sleep—knowing that in just a few hours, her precious daughter will be living 176 long miles away? Tears begin coursing down your face. You shake your husband awake.

"Honey, what are we going to do?"

"About what?" he asks blearily.

"Without Amanda around. What are we going to do?"

"Oh, we'll find something," he says with a sly wink.

He gives you a kiss and falls back to sleep. But you can't, so you get up, go down to the den, and look through photo albums of when she was little. Not the best way to stop the tears, Mom.

At eight the next morning, you are behind the wheel of your car, with your sleepy daughter in the seat next to you. You are pulling away from your house and following the 12 x 12 rental truck your husband is driving. Packed inside is everything Amanda needs for her physical and emotional comfort: her favorite pillows, a desk, her entire collection of stuffed animals, school clothes, social clothes (even some formal clothes), a television, three different sets of curtains, four bathrobes, seven pairs of pajamas, framed 5 x 7 photos of each one of her eighty-seven closest friends, and three bunches of inflated "Good luck, Amanda" Mylar balloons. The rest of her stuff is crammed into the backseat of your car.

The drive up is quiet; Amanda dozes off and on, while you pray that she won't be too lonely. Sure, she's a great kid, but she can be painfully shy at times; and going from a small high school to a university with 26,000 students can be overwhelming. You hope that it doesn't take too long for her to adjust.

A few hours later, your husband is on his third try at backing the U-Haul into a parking spot directly in front of Amanda's new dormitory. As you pull to the curb, you look over to your daughter to give her a final, reassuring "it's gonna be okay" smile. But she doesn't notice as she finishes touching up her lip gloss.

You watch your husband open the heavy rear doors of the truck. You know this is the part he is dreading; he hurt his back a month ago reaching under the sofa for the remote, and he's afraid today's heavy lifting could only make it worse. But he bends his knees into proper lifting position, reaches in, and bravely removes a lampshade. And then, as he heads for the dorm's entrance, a miracle happens.

Two young men—fit and handsome young men— approach your husband and ask if he needs some help unloading. He's thrilled and reaches for his wallet, but they wave him off. This one's on them, they tell him; it's their way of saying, "Welcome to the university."

You're overwhelmed by the good vibes you're feeling. You turn to share this with Amanda, but she is no longer in the car with you. Instead, she's headed toward her father and the two boys.

"Josh?" she calls to the blond one.

"Amanda!" he shouts back.

Your daughter smiles. The boys smile. Even your husband smiles, although he's not sure why. You, however, are unable to smile, because your jaw is resting on the floorboard.

As far as you knew, the only person Amanda knows on the whole vast campus is her roommate, Lacey. Although they've never met, they've been trading constant emails and photos about the perfect layout for their room. But how does your painfully shy daughter know this "Josh"? Could they have gone to high school together?

When you join the others and ask her about this, Amanda rolls her eyes and explains that no, Josh is from the northern part of the state. The two of them met on a university bulletin board designed for incoming freshmen.

Josh explains that he had to check into school two weeks early, because . . .

" . . . because he's on a lacrosse scholarship," Amanda finishes.

"Nice to finally meet you, Amanda," he says, extending his hand.

"Me, too," she responds, shaking his hand firmly.

Then Josh introduces his friend James, also a lacrosse player, and they explain that instead of holding practice today, their coach signed up the whole team to help incoming students get settled. And when he met Amanda online and found out it was just her mom and dad helping her, he thought it would make a perfect fit.

"Plus," Josh says to you and your husband, "Amanda's really funny." That's true, you think to yourself. But not that many people know it.

"Well, maybe we should get busy," your husband suggests.

"No, sir, you take it easy," James says. "Josh and I can handle it."

"That's right, Mr. Bowman," Josh says. "We heard you hurt your back, so don't you lift a thing, especially a remote."

Amanda stifles a laugh; your husband forces an embarrassed smile.

Josh and James unload the truck in less than an hour, and soon everything is placed in Amanda's room just the way she wants it.

While you and Amanda start putting her things away, your husband takes the two boys out for burgers.

When they return later, Amanda's things are put away and Amanda says that when Lacey checks in later and gets settled, it'll look like they've lived there forever.

The three of you walk onto the lawn in front of the dorm. Frisbees float, footballs sail, and another college year has begun. And now, as the late afternoon sun gets lower, it's time to say good-bye.

All of a sudden, your big, tough, "What's the big deal? She's just going away to college" husband is not so strong as you nudge him toward your daughter. "You know, sweetie," he finally says to her, "if you'd like us to spend the night, Mom and I could check into a motel and . . . "

"I'm fine," she tells him. "Besides, there's a football rally tonight. First game's next week."

Your husband just lowers his head.

"Daddy?" she says, lifting his chin and peering into his moistening eyes. "I love you."

And all he's able to muster is a nod and a huge hug.

Dang, now it's your turn.

You move to her and wrap your arms around her. "Mandy . . . " you start. But you can't continue.

Your daughter knows what's in your heart, because the same feelings are in hers. But if either of you say it, this might turn into a cry fest that could last the entire semester. And she doesn't want that to happen . . . shoot, she just touched up her eyeliner.

So she gently unwraps your arms and takes your hands in hers. "Dang, Mom," she says brightly, her eyes dancing from building to building, from Frisbees to footballs, from cyclists to skateboarders. "Can you believe it?! I'm in friggin' college!"

And the two of you laugh and twirl each other like third-graders.

Much later, you and your husband arrive home; it's been an exhausting day, but you're both too tired to go to bed. So he breaks open a nice pinot noir, and the two of you sip in silence. Yes, silence. No music blaring. No "ping-ping-ping" of her constant texting. No phone calls begging to stay out just a little later . . . Pleeeeeze?! Instead, you check your watch and wonder what she's doing at that very moment. Then your husband gets up and removes something from a bookcase. It's the same photo album from when she was little. As you page through it together, there are no tears.

But there are a lot of smiles.

★   ★   ★   ★   ★

Okay, now let's look at a scenario where every detail is exactly the same. Except for one thing: instead of a daughter, you have an eighteen-year-old son, Tim, who is headed off to college. He's scheduled to check into his on-campus dorm room at 12:30 P.M. on September 1.

At 8:00 A.M., you and your husband are loaded and ready to go, but your son isn't home. The 99 Cents store opened at seven, and there were some last minute items he desperately needed to guarantee that his college experience gets started on the right foot.

He finally gets home at 8:30 A.M. with nine pairs of sunglasses, three pounds of beef jerky, and two 12-packs of Starburst.

You don't get on the road until 9:15 A.M., because he had to finish packing. Your husband drives, you sit in the passenger seat, and Tim is in back, spread out and fast asleep. There's plenty of room for him, because all he's taking with him are two crammed duffel bags that are stuffed in the trunk. These two bags contain his entire supply of under-wear, T-shirts, jeans, and a deflated air mattress he's going to use in his dorm room for a bed because "beds take up too much room. Plus, you gotta make 'em!" Your darling son also had the presence of mind to pack four pairs of flip-flops, seven pairs of socks (three matching), his laptop, his Wii, and his cherished collection of naked lady bottle openers.

He did not, however, pack his skateboard. He feels that something that valuable is better carried under one's arm.

When you finally arrive at his dorm, he hops out of the car and tosses his duffel bags onto the sidewalk.

"Thanks, Mom, Dad," he says.

"Shouldn't we help you up to your room?" you ask as you and your husband get out of the car.

"No worries, Mom. I can handle it. Don't want to hurt Dad's back."

Then, as he reaches for one of his bags, a boy his age skateboards by. They look at each other with surprised familiarity. They engage in a conversation that goes like this (we've supplied an *adult translation* of their teen-speak in brackets):

"Dude?!" ("*I can't believe it. Jeff, is that you?*") says your son, surprised.

"Dude!!" ("*Tim!? Yeah, it's me. I didn't know you were going here!*") responds the other.

"Dude!" ("*Yeah, I'm going here. But I thought you were headed to Boston College.*")

"Dude . . . " ("*Too cold. I figured I'd stay closer to home, you know?*")

"Dude." ("*Good move.*")

When you inject yourself into this deep conversation, Tim introduces you to Jeff, who competed on a rival high school's debate team; apparently he and Tim went head-to-head several times over the years.

"This is one smart dude," your son says about Jeff.

"Duuuude," ("*Cut it out. You whipped my butt lots of times.*") Jeff responds.

"Dude," ("*Not as many as you whipped mine!*") Tim answers back quickly.

Then Jeff removes his meal plan card from his wallet and tells Tim that he's on his way to check out the food situation.

"Dude!" ("*I'm on the meal plan, too. And I am starved!*") Tim says, removing his wallet.

"Dude!" ("*Well let's go, bro!*") says Jeff.

Tim takes you and your husband aside for a quick group hug.

"Love you guys," he says.

He kisses you both, then hoists a duffel bag onto his shoulder and looks to Jeff. "Dude?" ("*Yo, I could use a little help with the other one.*")

"Dude," ("*No problem.*") Jeff says with a nod.

And then Jeff and your son head toward his dorm and soon disappear inside. You and your husband look at each other, shrug, and walk back to the car. You're home before dark.

You break open a bottle of Chardonnay, and the two of you sip in silence. Then your husband gets up and removes a photo album from the shelf. As you page through it, you realize that there aren't all that many pictures of your son in there.

That's because he's a second-born.

So you and your husband talk about some of the funny memories of your son as he was growing up.

You open a second bottle of wine.

Later that night, your husband tweaks his back again. But this time, the remote has nothing to do with it.

SIXTEEN

HERE'S NOT LOOKING AT YOU, KID

About a week after your child leaves for school, you will begin to adjust to your empty nest. If you have a daughter who's away, you now talk to her more than you did during all of her turbulent teen years put together. You discuss all manner of things—her classes, her friends, and her need for a car, even though she lives on campus and you spent $650 on a bike she just had to have before she left.

If your son is off at college, you will likely speak to him *less* than when he lived at home, and his phone calls will be more specific in nature: "Hey, Mom, do you know how to get transmission fluid out of a sofa cushion?" or "Hi, Mom . . . Listen, how high do you set the microwave to hard boil an egg?"

At about the two-week mark of your child being away, you will begin to treasure the peace and tranquility that moved into your house the exact moment that he or she moved out.

At the third week, you will begin reacquainting yourself with some of the little luxuries that existed in your life before the invasion of the little people:

- Sleeping late on weekends . . . with or without pajamas.
- Floating in the pool without cannon balls or "Marco! Polo!"
- Listening to *your* kind of music instead of punk and heavy metal bands. Hello, Barry Manilow; goodbye, "Bury Everyone."

- Watching *Antique Roadshow* instead of *Pimp My Ride.* Again, with or without pajamas.
- Entering the bathroom without needing a reservation. Or a book of matches.
- Knowing that a gallon of ice cream will last longer than an episode of *Sports Center.*

And best of all . . .

- You can see the future, and it belongs to you and your husband.

The two-month mark is generally when a temporarily child-free couple begins making changes to their home. These changes often begin in the garage, which has become a museum dedicated to the things your child has accumulated over the years. A large carton that's on top of what used to be your workbench is full of your daughter's fifteen-year-old ballet dresses.

The three bulky trash bags in the corner contain your son's shoulder pads, helmet, and other paraphernalia from the one season he played high school football, which was before he realized he wasn't a fan of pain. They occupy the space where your gardening tools used to be.

Like most men, your husband is impulsive and wants to toss everything, reasoning that it's highly unlikely that your daughter will ever audition for the Bolshoi or that your son will one day decide to try out for the Packers. But as a mom, you know better. You know that kids have a built-in "where's my stuff" detector that suddenly makes them desperately want whatever it is that you just threw out.

You should also know that dumping their stuff without asking can also create psychological havoc on a teenage mind that is not yet fully formed.

"Man," your eighteen-year-old says to himself when he finds out what you've done. "Mom chucked my Legos! Could I be next?"

This may help explain why a mother still keeps her thirty-seven-year-old daughter's high school cheerleading outfits neatly folded in two cedar chests in her garage, even though her daughter lives five hundred miles away and has told her mother that she has absolutely no interest in these outfits. Oh, I know you may think this mother is a crazy woman. And you may be right. In fact, you *are* right! I am going to get rid of those damn cheerleading outfits tomorrow. Or the day after—at the latest.

After you rearrange the garage, you can start making changes to your house. But a word of caution: Go gently, so you don't turn your child's world upside down. For example, if your child has been away at college for only six weeks, do not convert her bedroom into your own personal fitness center. Imagine her shock when she walks in and sees that where her bed used to be, there's now a treadmill and an ab cruncher. Where her dainty, shabby-chic dresser once stood, she sees a full array of intimidating free weights. And the Justin Timberlake poster that used to hang on the back of her door? Jane Fonda.

It's best to start with very slight, almost undetectable changes. Like on your kitchen counters, you might try switching the location of the toaster and the coffee maker. Not only will this give your child a very subliminal hint that other changes might be coming, it will also provide you with a great source of amusement as you watch your dean's-list eighteen-year-old holding two pieces of bread while staring blankly at the coffee pot.

Here's a timetable of acceptable changes you can make as your child matriculates through the college experience:

- Freshman (Year 1)—At least until spring break, keep big changes to a minimum, unless they're ones that your child is unlikely to notice. This means it's okay to hang new artwork, add bookshelves in the den, or paint your beige house a bright yellow.

- Sophomore (Year 2)—Remember that "sophomore" comes from the Greek for "wise fool." So although you've been able to fool your child with the slight changes you made during Year 1, you must remember that it's wise to keep it within reason during Year 2. However, because your child and twelve friends moved out of the dorm and into a two-bedroom apartment off campus ("Really, Mom, Dad . . . I'm just doing this to save you money"), it's likely that visits home will become less frequent. This means that you can be somewhat more ambitious, particularly in areas that pertain directly to you, but have virtually no effect on your children when they visit.

  Therefore, you can get a boob job, but not a full-time job. You can get a brand new convertible two-seater, but you cannot get rid of the old convertible sofa your child's friends sleep on. You and your husband can take French lessons, but please, no French kissing! Yech!

- Junior (Year 3)—This is a pivotal year for a couple of reasons. First, your child has been gone for two years and should be more comfortable with independent living. Second, the end of college is in sight, which equates to job hunting, a career, and an apartment of his or her own.

  At least that's the plan.

  All this translates into Year 3 being a good time for you and your husband to begin making long-term plans. Go ahead, call a contractor and get a bid on losing one of your kids' rooms so you can expand the master bedroom to include a fireplace and Jacuzzi. Or go online to research Tuscan farmhouses for when your husband finally takes his accrued vacation days, so you two can spend an entire summer in Italy. Or investigate opening that little boutique, just like the one you saw in Vermont fifteen years ago.

It is best, however, to keep these plans to yourself, at least for now. Because if you share them with your children—who are still of the age where their primary focus is on how *your* plans will affect *them*—they can sometimes rain on your parade.

"A new bedroom with a fireplace and Jacuzzi? And you couldn't afford to send me on Semester at Sea?" Or "Italy for the summer? You mean you're gonna be gone for my 21st birthday?" Or "Boutique? You're not going to be open at Christmastime, are you? Because I'll be home at Christmas."

- Senior (Year 4 . . . and 5 . . . and . . .)—With graduation finally in sight, parents grow increasingly excited. They feel proud. They feel relieved. And most of all, they feel all those tuition dollars coming back into their checking account. This is also when they begin asking their children about their plans after graduation.

Surely there are thousands of answers to this question. But in talking to hundred of moms, we came up with five that represent the most common. They're listed here, starting with the answer that pleases parents the most and moving down the scale to the one that makes parents scream . . . as they jump off a very tall building.

Q: "SO . . . WHAT HAVE YOU GOT LINED UP AFTER GRADUATION?"

Answer # 1: *"Well . . . I didn't want to say anything until I could take you guys out to a five-star restaurant to celebrate, but I just can't keep it inside any more. I GOT THE GREATEST JOB EVER! It's with a sports management firm, and I'll be working with some of the most famous athletes on the planet! The salary is amazing; I've got a two-year contract, company transportation, expense account, clothing allowance, and full health insurance. I went back for six different interviews, but I didn't say anything to you so you wouldn't get your hopes up. I start two weeks after graduation. I am so happy! Thank you for sending me to college. You are the most incredible parents ever."*

Answer # 2: *"Well, I didn't want to say anything until I could take you guys out to lunch, like at the Olive Garden or something, but yeah, I do have something lined up. I'm moving to New York City right after graduation . . . to pursue acting. Probably take a class or two, audition for Broadway shows. I've had good training in college, plus I've already got a lead on a bartending job right in the Theater District. And guess what? You remember Allison, right? The girl I brought home for Christmas and Easter? Well, she's moving to New York, too, and we've decided to live together. I know this is a shock, but Allison and I totally dig each other. And sure, it's expensive there, but we can handle it 'cause Allie just got a totally sweet job with some big sports management company."*

Answer # 3: *"Well, I didn't want to say anything until I . . . Are you guys hungry? I sure could use some breakfast."* (Then, forty-five minutes later . . .) *"Hey, that was great, you two, thanks. You can never go wrong at Denny's. Hey, Dad, c'mon, I've got this. Okay, but can I at least get the tip? All right, so here's what I wanted to tell you . . . I've thought a lot about it, and I want to apply to grad school. I've got the grades."* (Note to parents: "grad school" is interchangeable with "law school" and "med school." And although there's a little part of you that wishes your child would go out into the world and begin his life, you've always stressed the importance of education. And post–graduate work, no matter the field, is sure to earn respect from your friends.) Plus, the grad school he's considering is in another state. You begin researching student loans.

Answer # 4: *"Well, I didn't want to say anything until . . . Oh, there he is . . . Andy! Over here! Andy lives next door to the food co-op and sometimes gets free, two-day-old bagels. Hope you're hungry. Okay, here's the deal . . . Andy, me, Trevor, and Jeanine started a band, and we're pretty good. Trevor's dad owns a tool company, and he's got an extra van he can spare, so we're gonna tour! Look, I know a master's in environmental management is a really cool thing to have, and nobody can ever take that away from me. But hey, if I don't go for it now, I might always regret it, right? Hey, Andy, this is my mom and dad. Is that cream cheese safe?"*

Answer # 5: *"Well, I didn't want to say anything until you guys had eaten. Was the baloney and egg omelet okay? Sorry about the paper plates, but the dishwasher broke six months ago. Can I get you anything else? Okay, just let me know. All right, so about after graduation . . . With my degree, I have so many excellent options: business, research, teaching, launching a small start-up . . . So I think the best thing to do—in the interest of making a calm, informed decision—is to move back home. But only until I decide what's really right for me."*

So there you have it. Not everything goes according to plans.

The odds are overwhelming that one or more of your children will move back home after college . . . or even after a short, but promising, career. Or marriage.

So when they do, you will have to lay down an entirely new set of Mom Rules. Here are a few suggestions:

- I know you're used to living on your own, but now you're living on *my* own. So don't mess with me.
- You will do your own laundry unless you want to walk around with a very curious odor. Or naked.
- That squeegee in the glass shower that you always ignored? Ignore no more.
- The stainless steel, 4 x 4 box in the kitchen is called a dishwasher. Use it.
- Take the trash cans to the curb on Friday morning. Bring them back on Friday afternoon—the *same* Friday afternoon.
- When you come home late, do not block our cars by parking smack dab in the middle of the driveway. Be considerate and park your car on the street—in front of someone else's house.
- No, the dog you rescued in high school didn't stop pooping while you were away at college. Have a ball.
- Any articles of clothing lying on the floor for two straight days will be donated to the homeless shelter. If you persist in such messiness, so will you.

★　★　★　★　★

And as you lie in bed at night, listening to the television blaring from your college-graduate's bedroom, you can't help thinking about the plans the architect drew up for your new master bedroom with the Jacuzzi and fireplace.

But like the mom said, "Not everything goes according to plans."

SEVENTEEN

THE NEW MATH: 2 – 1 = 1 + 2

Like it or not, the current divorce rate in America hovers around 50 percent, which means there are a lot of single moms raising children. Add to this number the moms who have lost a spouse to death, as well as those moms who chose motherhood without feeling the need to have a husband or a partner, and it's not inconceivable that more than half the moms in this country are raising—or have raised—children on their own.

I know from experience that this is an amazingly difficult task, and when I see a single mom scurrying with her young kids, I often recall an incident from my own life. I was twenty-five, divorced, and the working mother of two daughters, aged five and two.

Like every weekday morning at 7:15, I was feeding the girls breakfast while scurrying to get dressed for work; contorting into my pantyhose, heating their cereal; finding a clean bra, pouring them juice; picking out a skirt, breaking up a food fight; ironing a blouse, pinning up their hair; throwing on some makeup, mopping up the bowl of cereal my older daughter knocked to the floor.

Finally, at 7:45, both girls were nicely dressed (two out of three ain't bad) and ready to head out the door. Although I had to get the younger one to the sitter, the older one to preschool, and me to work by 8:30, I felt I had time to spare . . . until the younger one used this opportunity to wet her pants, soaking the new outfit I'd just put on her.

We finally left our apartment at 8:00 and I knew I'd have to bend some traffic rules to make it to work on time. I worked for an insurance agent in his billing department, a completely boring and unrewarding job, and he was a boring and unrewarding boss who placed a high premium on punctuality, even though no one really started working until nine, because first we had to get our daily update on his golf game, his family, and the new, four-bedroom custom house he was having built.

I dropped my five-year-old off at preschool and was taking a shortcut to my two-year-old's sitter when she called out, "Mommy, fire engine!" Well, she was close: It was a policeman who was right on my tail, red lights flashing.

At 8:25, after a seven-minute lecture on driving safety and a $60 speeding ticket, I pulled away from the curb. Sixty dollars! Most single moms know that every penny is already spoken for, so after stopping at the sitter's, I spent the rest of my drive to work trying to figure out where I was going to find sixty extra dollars. Maybe if I held off on one of my credit card payments and canceled my Saturday night plans to have dinner and see a movie with my friend, Alice . . .

I arrived at work at 8:55, and as soon as I walked in the front door, I was met by my boss.

"So what's your story this time?" he asked.

I explained about the girls, and then the policeman.

"Well, I'd say your children are becoming a problem."

I felt the temperature of my cheeks go from 98.7 to what seemed like 124.5. "Problem?" I said.

"You are chronically late. I pay you to be here at 8:30."

"So take it out of my humongous check. My children are not a *problem*."

"I don't appreciate your tone," he said. "There are plenty of young ladies who would love to have your job."

"I'm sure there are," I said. "But before they could start, you'd have to get them all out of the nut house!"

Then he said some things that he didn't mean, and I said some things that I did.

At 9:16, I walked out of that insurance agency, jobless.

I went home, crawled into bed, and cried. What the hell was I going to do?

After two hours, I realized that self-pity was doing absolutely nothing for me or my girls, so I got up and grabbed the classifieds and the telephone.

At 2:15, I was sitting in a dentist's office. He was looking for someone to run his billing department, and in the course of the interview, he said I had a lovely smile. I suspect that in today's environment that would be a violation of some kind of law, but back then it was just a judicious compliment. After all, doesn't it make sense that a dentist would be apt to hire someone with a nice smile, rather than one who's teeth resembled a jack-o'-lantern's?

At 3:15, I walked out of the dentist's office with a job—a job that paid $50 more a week than my old one. And the best part? I didn't have to be there until 9:00!

So for all you single moms out there who are doing it on your own, keep faith. What you're doing is immensely important; and your kids appreciate it. Or will.

EIGHTEEN

DATING RULES FOR YOUR CHILDREN . . . AND FOR YOU

Statistics indicate that in 80 percent of divorce cases involving children, the mom is awarded primary custody of those children. Add to this the statistic that younger children have a habit of becoming older children, and you will see that it's quite likely for your house to become a two-generation hub of dating activity.

While this can be a healthy situation, it can also be complicated and stressful, because you, just like your child, are relatively new at this "dating" thing. Let's say you are forty-two and divorced four years ago; you didn't date for the first couple of years, because you had all you could handle with returning to the work force and trying to shepherd your child through this confusing and unsettling time. When you did start dating, you began cautiously and casually, preferring to start out with "safeties"—men you'd known for years who weren't a threat to take things where you didn't want to go. You dated men like your best friend's older brother, your cousin's neighbor, your cousin's business partner, your cousin.

Once you got your single legs back under you, you expanded your playing field to include anyone—except people you work with—which unfortunately disqualified that drop-dead handsome guy in marketing who's asked you out a couple of times, once for tennis, and once for dinner. These happen to be two of your favorite things, and it was very difficult to say "no." You're thankful he didn't mention "romantic, over-the-moon sex," because a hat trick is tough to resist.

Yet, you have more than just your needs to deal with, because you are now the mom of a full-blown teenager, hormones in overdrive, who is also beginning to date.

The first thing you do is talk to your child about respecting whomever they go out with, both physically and emotionally. Your child will likely be uncomfortable hearing this, but it's important you cover this territory on their first date. And it's even more important, on their second, third, fourth, and fifth dates.

You must also set strict curfews. But there is a caution here: When you set a time for your child to be home, and you happen to have a date that night yourself, you also need to be home by that time. But more importantly—because you're a mom—you must be home *alone*. In the living room. In your robe. Sipping tea.

As your child begins dating more, you will set other guidelines, and hopefully they will be obeyed without too much friction. But like so many other things we've discussed, the friction level will often depend on whether you're the mom of a teenage son or of a teenage daughter.

First, let's say you're the mother of Jack, a seventeen-year-old who has been dating for about a year. For the past couple of months, he's been going out exclusively with Molly, a girl in his class. Before every date, he asks for your fashion critique. And what's more, he generally follows it. This is because he is your son, a male, and you are his mom, a female, just like Molly. Before Jack leaves, he always tells you where they're going, which—thanks to cell phones—is a lot easier to confirm than it was when you were his age.

Ah, those were the days; lying to one's parents was so much simpler then.

Every so often, Jack brings Molly to the house to watch a movie, and you are always invited to join them.

When the shoe is on the other freshly pedicured foot and *you* have a date, Jack usually makes a point of staying around to meet the guy. Jack is always polite, but sometimes you can read his body language, which screams disapproval when he meets someone he doesn't think is right for you. As you feel your seventeen-year-old giving your suitor the once-over, you have this overwhelming feeling that you've seen this type of behavior before. Suddenly it occurs to you: It was your father . . . when he first met your ex.

And then one day it will happen: A man you've been dating invites you away for the weekend. God, you want to go; Kyle is a great guy. The two of you have a great time wherever you go. But you have to consider the feelings of Jack, the other man in your life.

There are two ways to approach it. First, if you want to keep your plans a secret, you can schedule your weekend away on a weekend that Jack will be spending with his father. That way, you can steal away as soon as Jack leaves, and get back on Sunday before he returns. But there's a huge risk in this ploy; the older Jack gets, weekends at his dad's have a way of changing. Jack may reschedule because of something going on at school. Or your ex may reschedule because of something going on with Tiffy, his twenty-seven-year-old wife who's pregnant with their triplets.

And who says karma doesn't exist?

But you decide to utilize your other option and tell Jack the truth, that Kyle invited you away for a weekend, but that you'll tell him "no" if Jack has a problem with it. Jack hears you out and sees that you really want to go.

"Problem? Mom, go and have a good time. I'll be fine here." You hug him and thank him, but before you call Kyle to accept his offer, Jack sits you down.

"Mom," he says seriously, "I want to talk to you about respecting Kyle both emotionally and physically . . . "

You both crack up. What a kid.

But before you start thinking you raised a saint, you should know that while you were on the phone in the kitchen with Kyle, Jack was on his cell phone with Molly.

"Guess what? Next weekend we have my house to ourselves."

★   ★   ★   ★   ★

All right, same exact situation, but a very different child. You are now the mother of a seventeen-year-old daughter, Jackie. It's a Friday night, and she hurries out of her bedroom, heading for the front door.

"See you later," she says perfunctorily.

"Whoa, whoa, whoa! Where are you going?"

"Jeff's here."

"Oh, he is? How nice. Who's Jeff?"

"A guy," she says, rolling her eyes impatiently.

"Really," you say. "A guy. I always thought 'Jeff' was a girl's name."

"Mom . . . "

"Is this Jeff ugly? Or maybe he doesn't know how to walk?"

"Mom, why are you being such a dork?"

"I can't think of any other reason why he wouldn't walk up and ring our doorbell. Then I would say, 'Good evening,' and then he would say, 'Hello, Mrs. Owens, my name is Jeff.

I'm here for Jackie.' And then I'd say, 'Oh, yes, Jeff. Please come in. Jackie will be out in a minute. She's changing.'"

"What's wrong with what I'm wearing?"

"Let's start with the skirt. If it were any shorter, you could wear the hem for a hat. Where did you get something like that?"

"In your closet."

Ooops.

Then the doorbell rings. You look at her.

"Now are you going to change that skirt or not?"

She says nothing, but responds with "The Pose," in which she straightens one leg—in this case, her right—and puts all her weight on it. This causes her right hip and her right buttock to jut out ever so slightly. Then she bends her left leg at the knee, so she resembles an ice skater performing a figure-4.

The final part of "The Pose" is actually two simultaneous moves: she folds her arms across her chest and squints her eyes in defiance.

With "The Pose," a teenage girl is saying, "Oh yeah? Make me!" Moms know this because they frequently used "The Pose" in their teenage years.

"Okay, fine," you say. "Let me put my hugging shoes on."

"Mom, no!"

You smile and start for the door.

"Mom, please?! No hugging . . . "

"Why? Hugs are nice."

"Not from a mom to a strange kid, they're not."

"Strange? Is Jeff strange?"

"Mom, please don't hug him, okay? It embarrasses me."

"Well, you in that skirt embarrass me."

You stare at her. She blinks. But she tries to stand her ground.

"Okay . . . " you warn, opening the door.

There stands Jeff, a neatly dressed, clean-cut kid. "Hi, Mrs. Owens. I'm Jeff and I . . . "

Before he finishes you say, "Jeff, of course!" Then you throw your arms open wide. But before you can hug him:

"Okay, okay!" Jackie calls as she hurries back into her bedroom.

You quickly close your arms and usher Jeff in. While your daughter is changing, the two of you chat and you find out they're headed to a movie and then for some pizza afterwards. Jeff has a 12:30 curfew.

"Jackie has to be home by midnight."

"No problem, Mrs. Owens," he says.

Then your daughter comes out of her room. She's changed into jeans, and Jeff's eyes light up when he sees her. And you understand why. She's growing into an attractive young lady. As they head out the door, you run and give her a big kiss.

She blushes and rolls her eyes.

After they pull away, you go into her room and retrieve your short skirt. A few minutes later, you're in front of your full-length mirror, trying to cram yourself into it.

Inhale . . . inhale . . . hold. You did it! And you know what? You still look pretty good in it. And if you relocate the button just a skosh, you'd actually be able to wear it and breathe at the same time.

It would be perfect to take with you next weekend when you go away with Kyle. He's already got the whole two days planned; tennis, dinners . . . You dropped that "no dating guys from work" thing months ago.

It should be wonderful weekend. You just wish it could be longer, but you can't leave until Jackie goes to her dad's.

NINETEEN

ACT YOUR (ELECTRONIC) AGE

You've probably already discovered that jumping back into the dating pool in your 30s and 40s is a lot different than when you started dating as a teenager. Back in the day, Donna Summer "Worked Hard for Her Money," Bananarama had a "Cruel Summer," and you were as "Footloose" as Kenny Loggins. At seventeen, you had all sorts of opportunities to meet guys; in fact, you didn't miss one of your high school's football games, because you had a huge crush on the quarterback.

But if you go to a high school football game now, you're probably checking out the quarterback's coach. Or his father.

Now that you have a child or two, a job, and a mortgage or rent, you have very little time—and even less energy—to party hearty. This probably explains why you see very few single moms in those spring break videos, but plenty of moms in video stores.

In your teens, you had ski trips in the winter, party-filled breaks in spring, and three-month vacations in summer.

But now, winter means your kids have ongoing runny noses, 3 A.M. coughing spells, and constant sore throats. And who has to take sick days from work to stay home and care for them? M-O-M.

Spring signals a week off from school for your kids, but income taxes and head-splitting allergies for you. But since you burned all your sick days during the winter, you can either cut into your vacation time, or sneeze and wheeze your way through April and May.

Then June rolls around, bringing summer with it. And of course, every single mom knows this means, "Ohmigod, school's out next week! What do I do with the kids?"

So for working, single moms, finding the time to date can be a chore. And as many of you have told us, meeting a nice guy to date can be a full-time job.

Without the benefits.

With kids at home, there are a lot of hurdles for working moms; babysitting issues make it difficult to be spur-of-the-moment. And even a well-planned night out with your girlfriends can sometimes put a big dent in the budget. Even "a quick drink after work" is oftentimes impossible because of day care/after-school care responsibilities.

So if a single, working mom is interested in meeting a man—for a serious relationship or otherwise—what's she to do?

First, there's a growing theory that when it comes to meeting the man you will eventually marry or couple with, there are only "three degrees of separation." This theory hypothesizes that most women meet their signifi cant other either through friends, or friends of friends.

We have no idea how true this premise might be; but just to be on the safe side, it's probably not a bad idea to have lots of friends . . . maybe, like, 100 thousand or so. But before you choose friends, make sure they have lots of friends, too. And it probably wouldn't hurt to lean toward friends/friends of friends who are smart, funny, attractive, financially stable, and breathing.

But making a lot of new friends can be difficult for a single working mom, unless she can do it while folding clothes, making lunches, or assembling the two-wheeler she bought for her six-year-old's birthday. And making *new* friends is particularly important for a mom who suddenly finds herself single, because she probably lost a number of her *old* friends in the divorce.

Take heart. After talking to single moms of all ages and dating experience, we heard two encouraging words over and over: the Internet.

There are hundreds of dating Web sites available these days; some, like match.com, chemistry.com, and eharmony.com, are for everyone. But there are hundreds of electronic matchmakers that are very specific. For example, let's say a woman lists herself like this: "I am a thirty-seven-year-old mother of two. I am a financially secure Episcopalian French-American heiress with homes in Easthampton and Aspen. I am looking for a twenty-nine-year-old Calvinist ski instructor who likes wining, dining, and children." As specific as this is, she will likely find her man. And when she does, she should also find a divorce lawyer better than her last one, who lost her homes in Zurich and West Palm Beach.

When Internet matchmaking services first appeared about fifteen years ago, many single women equated them with going on a blind date, which they further equated to "for losers only." And even those happy couples who did meet online seemed to be embarrassed to admit it.

"So how did you two meet?" someone would ask them at a party in 1995.

"Online," the guy would finally mumble apologetically, as if a more acceptable answer would have been, "We met in prison. She was a man back then."

Today, online dating seems to be *the* way for people—especially those over thirty-five—to meet. No doubt, the main reason for its popularity is its convenience. For a single, working mom, she can go online after she's put the kids to bed. It doesn't matter how her hair looks or what she's wearing. What's more, it's relatively inexpensive . . . certainly no more than dinner and a movie with friends.

We know several couples who met online and are blissfully together years later. And we've talked to a lot of single moms who are in various stages of relationships with men they've met through one of these Web sites.

For those who haven't yet tried this approach or are just starting out, here are some tips from experienced, Internet-dating moms . . .

Be Honest
It is a big mistake to make yourself something you're not. This means the photo you post should be no more than two years old. What's more, it should really be of you . . . not of your cuter, married, younger sister. And calling yourself a "world traveler" should be backed up by more than a high-school field trip to Mt. Rushmore and a weekend in Vegas, even though you breezed through the casinos of the Venetian; New York, New York; Paris; and the Monte Carlo.

There is, however, one thing you *can* fudge on a little bit—your age. But don't overdo it. Here is a very helpful chart—based on your actual age—to guide you on how much "year shaving" you can hope to get away with:

YOUR AGE	MAXIMUM DEDUCTION
25–30	6 months
31–40	1 year
41–50	2 years
51–60	3 years (4, with facelift, 4½ with boob job)
61–70	4 years (6, if potential mate has cataracts)
71–80	5 years (but only 2 if your hair has even a hint of blue in it)
81–90	As much as you want. Chances are, your date will forget what you told him. And so will you.
Under 25	Bitch!

Note: When using this chart, be sure to factor in the true ages of your children. For example, let's say you're a sexy, vibrant fifty-one-year-old mom. But because you've had a boob job and facelift, you take the recommended four-and-a-half-year deduction, which—as any woman knows—rounds out to seven years. So you've told your guy that you're forty-six. Then, at a Christmas party at your place, he meets your thirty-two-year-old daughter. He does the math and determines that either 1) You've been lying to him the past fifteen months, or 2) You had a child when you were eleven. Either of these could torpedo any possibility of the two of you singing "Auld Lang Syne" together anytime soon.

Choose a Proper Screen Name

For the uninitiated, patrons of these Web sites do not use their real names. There are a couple of reasons for this. If you use your real name, an interested suitor could call you at home and bug you mercilessly until you agree to go out with him or until you obtain a restraining order. Also, if your real name doesn't necessarily imply worldliness or romance, you're already at a disadvantage and will likely only receive inquires from the Dickie Dummtzhits of the world.

You need to give careful consideration to your screen name so that it accurately reflects the essence of you, while at the same time catches the eye of men who share your sensibilities.

For example, if you're a mom who's a poetry buff, something like "ShkspreLvr" might be an appropriate screen name. However, "WntaLongfellow" . . . maybe not so much. Or say you're a professional photographer. Perhaps "Pix4All" wouldn't be bad; "IXpose4U" probably would.

Be Selective

Choosing a proper screen name is also important when it comes to determining whether a male candidate might be good dating material. For example, let's say you're perusing your dating Web site when you notice a picture of a guy you haven't seen before. God, is he handsome! You go over his stats and he's like . . . *perfect!* He's a few years older than you (maturity is a wonderful quality), divorced for six years (excellent—plenty of time to get over the whining), has two kids (ah-ha: fathering experience), and is the national sales rep for a well-known women's clothing manufacturer (make room in your closet, girlfriend!). Among his hobbies he lists reading (what a coincidence—you can read, too!), golf (how hard could that be to learn?), but his main passion is breeding thoroughbred racehorses (ka-ching!).

You're about to respond when you notice his screen name: "Stallion4U."

Beware! Do you really want to go out with a forty-seven-year-old man who calls himself a stallion? And consider this: If he's such a stallion, how come he doesn't already have a mare in his barn?

Why didn't he just go with "ImaJerk"?

There are some other red flags you should be aware of when reviewing a man's picture and profile.

Pictures: Be suspicious of a guy whose picture shows him standing next to any type of motor vehicle. This usually means that he knows he's nothing special, but figures his 1976 Trans-Am just might win you over.

Also, if a candidate is jauntily seated on his Harley Davidson, his vibe is probably, "Hey, Mama, let's go cruising." But do you think he's ever going let you get behind the handlebars? C'mon. So you need to ask yourself if this guy is so irresistible that you're willing to spend two weekends a month on three-hundred-mile motorcycle trips. Remember, he'll be in the pilot's seat, the open highway ahead of him and the wind in his face, while you spend five hours staring at the back of his sweaty, hairy neck.

If so, hop on, "Mama."

It's also a good practice to be leery of any man who wears more jewelry and shows more cleavage than you do.

Profiles: Obviously, men like to put themselves in the best light so that attractive, intelligent women like you will give them the time of day. And if all goes well, the time of night. But in attempting to impress you, men don't always tell the truth, the whole truth, and nothing but the truth. This is not say that they lie; it's that they will use certain words, phrases, and terms in their profiles to make themselves seem more desirable. These might appear innocent at first glance, but a closer look might prove otherwise. Here is a short glossary to show that a man's profile may not always accurately describe the man himself:

HIS WORDS	MEANING
"5 feet 11½ inches tall"	Trying too hard to be a 6-footer. He likely tops out at 5' 7", even in his disco shoes.
"consultant"	Between jobs
"self-employed"	Out of a job
"philosopher"	Never had a job
"adores animals"	12 cats, 3 dogs, and an iguana
"love late-night walks"	Insomniac
"love to watch the midnight moon dancing on the water."	Insomniac with a boat
"wine connoisseur"	Will horde the wine list so you can't select a bottle over $12.00
"great sense of humor"	Will mortify you with his non-stop jokes to waitresses and his impersonation of Mike Tyson fighting Adam Lambert
"My best friend? My mom."	Lives with her
"I'm a fitness nut."	Wears spandex shorts to the beach

HIS WORDS	MEANING
"I'm a Renaissance man."	Likes going to restaurants that feature knights on horseback
"I'm a writer."	Insane
"I'm into the arts."	TiVo's *Dancing with the Stars*
"I like to travel."	Lives in a camper on the back of a pickup
"I want a meaningful relationship."	"If we're not in the sack by 10, ciao, baby."

★　★　★　★　★

And now, a final word about moms and Internet dating—and this story comes to us from our friend, Arlene, and her daughter, Kristen, who was two weeks shy of eighteen and in her senior year of high school. Arlene had been divorced for three years, and had been dating off-and-down for the last year or so. It was a Saturday night, and Arlene had a first date scheduled with a man named Jim, who was picking her up at 7:30.

At 7:20 when her doorbell rang, Arlene went to answer it, expecting it to be Jim. But before she reached the door, Kristen came tearing out of her room.

"That's for me," Kristen said.

"No, I think it's for me," Arlene insisted.

"Mom!" Kristen said impatiently, elbowing her way past her mother and opening the door.

Standing on the front porch were two men: Jim, about forty-five, in slacks and a sport coat, and Dalton, about 20, with long, shaggy hair, several tattoos, and wearing black from head to toe. Jim was a CPA. Arlene suspected that Dalton wasn't.

"Jim," Arlene said to Jim.

"Dalton," Kristen said to Dalton.

"Come in," Arlene said to Jim.

"Let's go," Kristen said to Dalton.

"Wait a second," Arlene said to her daughter. "Aren't you going to introduce us?"

Kristen sighed. She just wanted to get out of there because she knew what was coming next.

"Mom, Dalton. Dalton, my mom," she said quickly. "Okay, bye," Kristen said, trying her best to get out of there.

"Do you go to school with Kristen?" Arlene asked Dalton.

"No, I graduated high school a few of years ago," he said with bemusement.

"Oh, I see," Arlene said with a forced smile. "Kristen, could I see you in the kitchen for a minute?"

"Mom . . . "

"Kristen, kitchen!" And then she added, "Be right back, Jim," as she dragged her daughter from the room.

"Okay, how old is this Dalton, and how do you know him?" Arlene asked once they were alone.

"He's twenty; he goes to NYU, and what does it matter how I know him? We're just friends."

"You're just friends with lots of people your own age. And you're not going out with them. How come I've never met this Dalton before?"

"Because I've never met him before."

"What?"

"We met online, Mom. What's the big deal?"

"What's the big deal?" You can't go out with someone you've never met before.

"Why?" snarled Kristen. "*You* are."

"What?" Arlene felt flush.

"I know you met that Jim on eHarmony."

"That's ridiculous," Arlene answered ridiculously.

"Mom, I heard you talking to Aunt Carol the other night about how nervous you were about meeting him face-to-face for the first time."

Arlene studied her daughter for a moment. "You know, it's not polite to eavesdrop."

"Eavesdrop? Mom, you were giggling like a schoolgirl."

"Look, what I do has nothing to do with you. Jim and I have spent lots of time talking and emailing."

"So have Dalton and I. He's majoring in psychology, which is what I want to do. And we both like a lot of the same things—like old horror films. That's where we're going tonight."

"But the tattoos . . . " Arlene said.

"Mom, you have a tattoo on your ankle."

"That doesn't count; I was eighteen with too much Cuervo in me."

"Well, Dalton doesn't have that excuse, because he doesn't drink."

"But he's so much older than you."

"Two years. Jim's at least that much older than you are."

"No he isn't; he said he's forty-five," Arlene said. Then she added, "You really think he's older?"

"Mom, the guy's fifty if he's a day. But so what? If he's nice and you have fun with him . . . " She felt her mother wavering. "So how come you can go out with a guy you've never met, and I can't?"

"Okay," Arlene sighed. "Where are you going again?"

"The Odeon," Kristen said. "They're running a restored version of *The Blob*."

"I want you home at 12:30," Arlene said.

"And I want you home by 1:00," Kristen said with smile.

Then they exchanged a quick hug and went off to meet the men they'd never met before.

As a postscript, the whole Internet dating thing turned out happily for both Kristen and Arlene. Because now, eight years later, Arlene is blissfully married to a wonderful man named Patrick, whom she met at the wedding of a mutual friend's daughter.

But wait a minute . . . What about Jim? He and Arlene dated several times, and although they had fun, they both soon recognized that whatever "it" is, it wasn't there for them. They still talk occasionally, usually around the holidays. Jim is still out there, trying to find Mrs. Right.

So what did Internet dating have to do with Arlene's happiness?

Well, Kristen and Dalton have been ecstatically married for three years. Dalton is a clinical psychologist working with troubled and at-risk youths, and Kristen is working on her dissertation for her doctorate as well. But that's on hold for a few months, because in just six short weeks . . .

Arlene is going to be a grandmother!

TWENTY

TURN OUT THE LIGHTS...

And now, some Mom Rules for you to take home as parting gifts:

Don't over-equip yourself when going out with the baby. Diapers and wipes and snacks. Done.

If you stay calm, baby stays calm.

It's okay for kids to skip school for travel. Travel opens their eyes and minds.

You're never too old to play tag or hide-and-seek with your kids.

If you allow yourself to laugh at your mistakes, you'll have a happy life.

If your child throws a tantrum in public, it's okay to shout out, "Does anyone know whose child this is?"

Before you allow your child to drive, make sure he/she knows how to change a tire.

When your child has his/her heart broken, there's no better medicine than a hug, a kiss, and a cup of hot chocolate with marshmallows.

Allow your kids to "play" sports; those who want to "work" at them, will.

When your child does something stupid, make sure you don't.

If your child seems lost, you can be the roadmap.

It's easy to raise a perfect child; it's kids like yours who make life interesting.

When you think no one appreciates you, watch your child sleeping.

If you open a door for your child, she or he will do the same for others.

When your child misbehaves, sometimes a tickle beats a time-out.

Before you say, "Go ask your father," remember that at a party last night, this is the man who insisted on showing everyone how he could burp the alphabet . . . backwards.

It's hard to take life slower on a diet of fast food.

You can lead your son to water, but you can't make him wash behind his ears.

You can lead your daughter to water, but you can't make her get in unless she thinks she looks really good in her new bathing suit.

When you feel like you're being pulled in all directions, take the route that leads to the Häagen-Dazs.

If at first you don't succeed, blame your husband.

When your child receives applause, make sure your hands aren't the ones clapping the loudest.

Since children are a gift, we should be able to return them.

When everything is cruising along, remember the Titanic.

The best "I love you, Mom" comes when you least expect it.

Children are sponges. They pick up everything you say, and they work better with soap.

Children should be seen and not heard . . . especially when they start trumpet lessons.

If you think you've heard it all, just wait until you ask your seven-year-old why he decided the cat needed a haircut.

Don't be over-protective. Let kids do what kids do best—climb trees, pop wheelies, jump off walls, eat food off the floor.

Be sure you live close to a good E.R.

And finally, the Mom Rule that trumps all others comes from our pal Cindy Glazar, mother of two:

Mom is always right. If everyone in the household acquiesces to this rule, then lots of time is saved each and every day.

Hopefully you've had a few chuckles along the way to seeing that being a mom *is* the best job in the world, as well as one of the most challenging. But even with everything you do—the comforting, the driving, the supporting, the feeding, the nurturing—we're sure there are times you ask yourself, "Does anyone notice?" Do your kids appreciate all the things—big and little—that you do for them? Well, rest assured, they do. If you think not, just read some of the things children—from four to forty-three—wrote about their moms:

My mom rules because she brings me soup and crackers whenever I'm sick. Even when she knows I'm faking.

My mom rules because she's energetic and has a mohawk.

My mom rules because she doesn't know that when we have peas for dinner, I feed mine to the dog.

My mom rules because she always smells good, except sometimes after she plays tennis.

My mom rules because she always makes my bacon just perfect.

My mom rules because she doesn't have lumps in her pancakes. Or anywhere else.

My mom rules because she keeps good secrets.

My mom rules because she sawed down a Christmas tree.

My mom rules because she drives fast, even when she's lost.

My mom rules because when we go to church, she lets me give the man the money.

My mom rules because she lets me play in the rain, but not when it's too cold.

My mom rules because she can hold her breath for a whole minute.

My mom rules because she beats my dad at Jeopardy almost every night.

My mom rules because when my grandma died, she made her whole speech without crying once.

My mom rules because she fixed a dent in her car before my dad knew about it.

My mom rules because she can text as fast as my sister.

My mom rules because sometimes when she puts me to bed, she rubs my head until I fall asleep.

My mom rules because the only time she makes us eat pork chops is on my dad's birthday.

My mom rules because sometimes she cries when she laughs.

My mom rules because she taught me how to ski when I was three.

My mom rules because when I had my operation, she slept in the hospital with me.

My mom rules because my friends say I have the nicest mom of anyone.

And lastly, our forty-three-year-old friend, Gail, told us:

My mom rules because—even after the huge pain I was growing up—she still loves me even more! Can you believe it?

Of course we believe it.

'Cause that's what moms do.

ACKNOWLEDGMENTS

To Dionn and Ron Avant, Mischon and Kevin Beneda, Nick Bertino, Mary and Ken Binning, Patti and Dave Coulter, Tami Enzistaga, Jeri and Joe Gesto, Cindy Glazar, Shannon Goar, Mimi Gross, Beth King, Jody McIntyre, Ann Sayre, Carolyn Schmidt, J.B. Whitney, and Larry Balmagia, and all the moms (and dads) who shared their stories with us, thank you very much.

To Zip and Denise Vitullo: You are truly our ports in any storm. A thousand thanks.

To our friends at Skyhorse, Mark Weinstein and Julie Matysik. Mark, thanks for the opportunity to do yet another for you. And Julie, we so appreciate your smooth and insightful editing. We hope we can do it again soon.

To Dan Lazar at the Writers House: You are, and continue to be, the best.

To our moms, Alice Cutler and Carolyn Milligan.

And finally, to moms everywhere. You rule for so many reasons.